C000140476

How to make

your case in the media

EXISTING TITLES IN THE
HELPING HAND BOOK SERIES:

HOW TO WRITE THE PERFECT PRESS RELEASE
Real-life advice from editors on getting your story in the media

HOW TO BUILD A WINNING BID TEAM
Practical advice to improve key skills that help you win
more business

HOW TO WRITE WELL AT WORK
Simple steps to get you writing with fluency and confidence

HOW TO MAKE YOUR CASE IN THE MEDIA
The complete guide to getting your message across in the press
and on radio and TV

All available from
www.helpinghandbooks.co.uk

HOW TO MAKE

YOUR CASE IN THE MEDIA

The complete guide to getting your message across
in the press and on radio and TV

PETER BARTRAM

AND

COLIN COULSON-THOMAS

A Helping Hand Book
from
New Venture Publishing

First published 2006 as a Helping Hand Book
Second edition revised and enlarged 2008
by New Venture Publishing Ltd
© Peter Bartram and Colin Coulson-Thomas 2006 and 2008

All rights reserved. No part of this book may be reproduced, stored in a retrieval system
or transmitted in any form by any means, electronic, mechanical, photocopying, recording,
scanning or otherwise, except under the terms of the Copyright, Designs and Patents Act
1988 or under the terms of a licence issued by The Copyright Licensing Agency Ltd,
90 Tottenham Court Road, London W1T 4LP UK (www.cla.co.uk),
without the written permission of the publisher.

The moral right of the authors has been asserted.

This book sets out to provide accurate information and general advice on the subject
matters covered. It is published in good faith, but neither the publisher nor authors
can accept liability for loss or expense as a result of relying on particular statements
in the book. This book is sold on the clear understanding that the publisher is
not involved in providing a professional service. If in doubt about any particular
circumstances, readers are advised to seek reliable professional advice before taking any
action based upon information provided in this book. Parts of this book were originally
published as *The Complete Spokesperson* by Policy Publications.

New Venture Publishing Ltd
29 Tivoli Road, Brighton
East Sussex BN1 5BG

E-mail: info@newventurepublishing.co.uk
www.helpinghandbooks.co.uk

ISBN: 0-9552336-3-1
978-0-9552336-3-0

British Library cataloguing-in-publication data
A catalogue record for this book is obtainable from the British Library

Cover design by Mark Tennent
Typeset in Caslon by Mark Tennent, Worthing, West Sussex
Printed and bound by One Digital, Brighton, East Sussex BN2 4AA

About the authors

Peter Bartram is an experienced editor, business writer and journalist who has contributed to a wide range of newspapers and magazines and has written 18 books. His other titles for New Venture Publishing include *How to Write the Perfect Press Release*, *How to Build a Winning Bid Team* (with Carol Kennedy) and *How to Write Well at Work*. During a long career in journalism, he has interviewed thousands of individuals – from people in the street to political party leaders, from shop-floor workers to the chief executives of multinational corporations. He can be contacted at peter.bartram@journalist.co.uk or via www.newventurepublishing.co.uk

Colin Coulson-Thomas, Professor of Direction and Leadership at the University of Lincoln, is an experienced media spokesman and chairman of award winning companies. He is a Fellow of the Chartered Institute of Public Relations – one of seven fellowships of professional institutions that he holds – and has authored more than 30 books and reports. These include *Winning Companies; Winning People* (Kingsham Press, 2006) and *The Knowledge Entrepreneur* (Kogan Page, 2003). Colin Coulson-Thomas has helped more than 100 boards to communicate more effectively and improve performance. He has reviewed the processes and practices for winning business of more than 100 companies and has spoken at more than 200 national and international conferences and corporate events in more than 20 countries. He can be contacted at colinct@tiscali.co.uk or via www.coulson-thomas.com.

CONTENTS

Checklist of checklists

Chapter 1

Any comment?

This is a book for people who suddenly find they have to face the media. It's also a book for people who've already had a brush with the media, perhaps weren't happy with the outcome – and want to perform better next time around. And it's for the public relations consultants who help clients put across their messages to the media. In short, a book for spokespeople and their advisers.

It's not a book that troubles too much about theory. There are plenty of those already. Instead, it's a book for people who want practical advice about how to put their case to print or broadcast journalists in the most compelling and convincing way. It's full of practical advice and there are no fewer than 67 checklists that distil much of the advice into a readily useable form. So this is a book to read now and keep for future reference.

With that said, let's get started.

One of the strengths of an open society is that everybody is entitled to put their point of view.

Yet one of the weaknesses is that not everybody is well-equipped to do so. Some individuals are natural talkers, skilled debaters, forceful proponents of whatever case it is that they want to argue. Others are less eloquent, tongue-tied even. Or, maybe, they don't have the broader vision to take a step back and look at how they can put their case most effectively – perhaps to a public that is sceptical, even hostile.

There are, of course, an infinite number of situations in which a spokesperson could be called on to put an organisation's case. They range from a major national press conference where one or more spokespeople could address a hundred or more print and broadcast journalists to a single person meeting the reporter from the local paper to have a chat about a parochial development. There may not seem to be much in common with both of those very different situations.

In fact, both situations – and all the ones in between – have two factors in common. The first is that they involve somebody putting their case across in words but also (as we shall discover) in more subtle ways by the attitudes and behaviours they adopt and the impression they leave behind them. The second is that the message they've given will be conveyed through the good or malign offices of journalists (whichever way you choose to look at it) to the readers of newspapers and magazines, the listeners of radio programmes, the viewers of a growing number of television channels and, increasingly, the surfers of websites and other digital media. Or, of course, some or all of them.

In other words, the work of the spokesperson is to convey a message through the filter of a tough, maddening, sceptical, cynical, sometimes humorous, competent (or, rarely, incompetent), slice of the population known as journalists. The purpose of this book is to give you some suggestions about how you can do it so that it goes right – and serves your organisation's objectives – more often than it goes wrong.

But isn't this something that should be left to public relations professionals?

Up to a point.

Public relations professionals have a lot to offer organisations that are trying to put their case in the media more effectively. They can advise on strategy, on the range of media available, on ways to access it and they can bring their creativity to bear on devising ways to put the organisation's message across in words and images. But despite all this, somebody has to stand up and speak to journalists.

It can't be avoided. Journalists are used to working with PR people and know well their skills (and, it has to be said, their occasional limitations). But sooner or later – and it's usually sooner – journalists want to hear the message from the principal's mouth. There is nothing more frustrating for journalists than to get the sniff of a good story through PR channels only to discover there's nobody available from the organisation in question to speak about it. So developing spokespeople is a critical element of any successful public relations campaign.

Those organisations that succeed best are often those where the spokesperson (or spokespeople) are most enthusiastic about their role. Indeed, some organisations have found an excellent way to get a stream of good coverage for themselves is by turning a chosen spokesperson into a "guru" – the kind of expert journalists seek out at short notice when they want instant comment on a breaking story or deeper insights into a developing one.

So much of what follows in succeeding chapters focuses on how PR professionals and an organisation's spokespeople can work together to deliver the kind of teamwork which produces positive media coverage.

And yet even those who've had experience of being a spokesperson in the past could have much to learn for the future. For the fact is that the role of the spokesperson is changing in the face of two global trends. The first is a growing movement in many parts of the world to demand the "right to know" and the second is the development of more and different media channels. We can get some clues as to the kinds of skills spokespeople of the future will need by exploring both of these trends.

People didn't always feel they had the right to know. Step back only a few decades in the UK and you discover a deferential society in which people were generally more willing to accept what they were given (in information as well as material goods) and where there was a more finely-tuned sense of privacy. This was the world in which newsreaders wore dinner jackets (even on the radio) and where television interviewers would no more think of asking a searching question than sticking their tongue out at the camera.

In this climate, it was much easier for organisations to control the flow of information to the media. The media were less willing to challenge, more prepared to accept what they were given. The concept of the "investigative journalist" was yet to appear on the British scene. The interface between organisations of many kinds – in business, the public authorities and elsewhere – was less confrontational. Spokespeople were less likely to be ambushed by the unexpected question. Usually, they expected and received an easy ride.

There was never one moment when everything changed. Probably the tide started to turn in the late 1950s when television interviewers, such as Robin Day, began to take a more robust approach to dissembling politicians and evasive business people. It sent a signal that the great and the good (and the not-so-great and not-so-good) didn't always have to be handled like new-born chicks. The tide bore on during the 1960s with pioneering journalism, such as *The Sunday Times'* Insight team, which developed the concept of in-depth newspaper investigations, and the appearance of television "chat shows" in which famous or important people (and people who thought they were famous or important) were brought into television studios and treated with as much decorum as an irritating neighbour who'd popped round for a natter.

By the start of the 1970s, the old deference of many journalists was all but dead and there was a new spirit of enquiry abroad in both newspapers and broadcasting – a spirit which spokespeople had to take into account in the way in which they dealt with the media. True, there were still redoubts of secrecy, such as the public sector, but they were gradually broken down as, for example, local council committee meetings were opened by law to the press and, in recent years, the Freedom of Information Act provided public access to facts that might otherwise have lain undisturbed in public servants' files.

Now, far from deference, there are many journalists – and not only on the major national newspapers and broadcasting stations – who regard it as their duty to question, even provoke, those who have information they want to publish. The game has changed with the old rules abandoned and it's not so much that the new game has no rules as that nobody is quite sure what they are.

The second big trend which spokespeople have had to take on board is the development of new media channels – a development that is still in full flood. Back in the age of deference, there was one, then two, then three television stations which broadcast for limited hours each day, plus three then four national radio stations. It is true that there were more national and regional newspapers – as late as the early 1960s, London still had three evening newspapers – but the newspapers were much smaller than they are today. There were far fewer magazines than there are now – and they were also smaller in pagination.

All this meant that there were strictly limited opportunities for spokespeople to get their messages across. Only large and important organisations usually got much of a chance. Thousands of lesser organisations that would have liked their 15 minutes of fame were left unreported. But as the number of television and radio stations grew (the latter especially through the innovation of local radio) and newspapers became fatter, more spokespeople found their way into the big publicity tent. The proliferation of consumer, business, and trade and technical magazines also opened up a whole range of new publicity opportunities for organisations of all kinds.

And, just as it looked as though organisations were spoilt for choice of potential media, along came the digital revolution. This has opened up a whole range of new ways for spokespeople to reach their audiences, sometimes through bypassing the intermediary of journalists – for example, via websites, e-mails and web conferences.

In fact, the media explosion has been so great the nature of the problem for spokespeople has now reversed itself. In the old days, with limited media, the problem for many organisations was finding a way to get their voice heard. Now, the nature of the problem is not so much getting an opportunity to put your case – there are so many opportunities – as making it stand out from the millions of messages that pour out from all these media every day.

The question is: how do you get your message noticed?

The medium, Marshall McLuhan told us, is the message. But it's probable that even the guru of communications, writing in the 1960s, wouldn't have realised just how much his perceptive thought would shape the way people approached the business of getting their messages across in the media in the years ahead. The rise of visual media, principally television, put a premium on image and downgraded the significance of substance.

When serious newspapers would think nothing of running three thousand words on a subject, there was room for people to make their case in detail – to develop the logic of their argument from point to point, to illustrate with telling examples or references, to reach a rounded conclusion. Today, serious newspapers rarely run pieces at that length – except in magazine supplements – and the most pervasive of mediums, television news, often deals in the "sound bite", where a complex point of view may need to be distilled into a single sentence.

Is it any wonder that the rise of television and popular media has been accompanied with the emergence of the "spin doctor", a derogatory phrase designed to describe an individual skilled at twisting a case to present it in the best possible light, irrespective of the facts? Let's be clear: there is nothing wrong with presenting a case in the best possible light. But there is much that is wrong in distorting the truth – either by twisting facts or suppressing essential information – in a way that leaves an audience with a misleading impression. Such an approach may score short-term tactical advantage but, when the deception is discovered – and, these days, with such a pervasive and inquiring media, the deception is almost always discovered – it results in a long-term strategic disaster, the loss of trust. If the people who are listening to what you have to say don't trust you, you might as well save your breath.

In fact, trust is the new secret weapon for the spokesperson of the future. The explosion of media channels means there is plenty of room for people from many backgrounds to express different points of view – perhaps contrary to those you would want to put across. And people are more cynical. They're less easily convinced than they would have been in a more deferential age. Today, an organisation and its spokespeople have to earn trust – and the way to do it is to use the truth, the whole truth and nothing but the truth.

It doesn't hurt to look and sound like a human being either. The robotic metronome who sounds as though he (or she) has been sent out to repeat an official line is an immediate turn-off for most people. The fact is that people warm to other people who seem to have the best qualities of themselves – humanity, empathy, generosity of spirit. Spokespeople who get known as warm human beings have scored even before they've opened their mouths.

So when McLuhan said the medium is the message, he was only partly right. We seem to be moving into a new age where the message is becoming more important – not only to organisations that want to put their case to the public at large (or parts of it) but to those charged with the task of acting as their spokespeople. But what message? A good starting point is to understand what it is, exactly, that the media want. And to do that, you must turn to the next chapter.

Chapter 2

Stalking the media

Sometimes the media will come after you. And, sometimes, you'll wish they hadn't. Because they may be probing into topics that you'd rather not talk about. When that happens it's important not to lose your cool and, if it's a problem you fear, you'll find plenty of advice on how to deal with crises in chapter nine.

But, sometimes, you will be pleased that the media are seeking your views. Because, in that case, the fact they want to know what you think means you've established yourself personally, or your organisation, or perhaps both, as a useful source of media information and comment.

However, there are plenty of organisations that don't get the media attention they believe they deserve. Why does the press always write about our rivals? may be a plaintive question voiced in the boardroom. In many cases, the answer to that question will lie in the fact that the rivals are far better at stalking the media and providing them with interesting stories they want to write or broadcast about.

Often, the job of approaching the media with proactive messages (of the kind you'll find more about in chapter three) falls to the public relations professionals. But there is no reason why it has to be. If you have an interesting story to tell, there will usually be a journalist somewhere who would like to hear about it. The problem is that many organisations – public authorities, not-for-profit organisations as well as both listed and private companies

– are so desperate to win their share of coverage they bombard the media with information which is simply never going to make it into print or onto the airwaves.

The untold story of the interchange of information between organisations and the media, is that many editors, broadcasters and journalists are becoming increasingly irritated by the avalanche of hopeless story ideas which flood their e-mail in-boxes. When you're seeking useful and productive media coverage, quality counts. Winning those vital column inches is not a matter of sending journalists a mountain of unwanted information, but of targeting them with the kind of stories that it's likely they might want to write about.

Number of pitches editors receive

As part of the research for the second edition of this book, we set out to ask editors what it is they're looking for when it comes to receiving "pitches", as they're usually called, from PR people. (A "pitch" really means sending an idea to journalists to see if they're interested in writing about it. Sometimes PR professionals also talk about "selling in" stories.) We collected information from 75 editors and senior journalists. They include journalists who write for national newspapers, editors of regional dailies and weekly newspapers, writers on famous bookstall magazines, and editors from business and professional publications as well as the trade and technical press. So, a good cross-section of journalists.

We found that the average journalist receives no fewer than 51 pitches a week from PR people and others. This figure breaks down into 22 offers of contributed articles, 16 requests to interview somebody and 13 invitations to press conferences, briefings or other events. At this point, it's worth giving a health warning. Journalists don't sit around counting the number of pitches they receive from PR people. So the figures they gave us were, necessarily, estimates. Even so, we can accept these estimates as reasonably accurate, based on the fact that the flow of "pitches" to individual journalists tends to be consistent and fairly constant.

The average is 51. But, of course, nobody is average. Some receive massively more than the 51 pitches, while others receive fewer. So, for example, the editor of a Sunday newspaper who took part in the research says he receives around 675 pitches a week, of which roughly 300 are offers of contributed articles and a further 300 requests to interview somebody.

The editor of a national monthly business magazine reckons to receive around 600 pitches a week, including 250 contributed article offers and 250 interviews. Even a weekly newspaper has around 100 offers a week, including 40 contributed articles and 10 interviews. It also gets invitations to about 50 events a week, far more than its reporting staff can possibly cover. And so it goes on. Even a famous bookstall magazine which never carries contributed articles – it's solely written by its own journalists – is getting 15 offers of articles a week. If you're after media coverage, it makes no sense to offer journalists something they don't want because they never use it.

The sad fact is that many of the organisations who habitually complain that they don't get the media coverage they feel they deserve fail on a number of counts to offer the media what it wants. Or they do so in ways which make it difficult for the media to take advantage of what they have to offer – like the people who offer contributed articles to the magazine that doesn't publish them.

There has to be a better way. And the better way is to avoid the ten worst mistakes that are made when offering ideas to the media.

When collecting information from the 75 editors and journalists, we asked them about the main reasons they turned down ideas offered by PR professionals and others. We wanted to find out what was going wrong as a first step in helping people to put it right. To get some idea of how serious the reasons for turning down ideas were, we asked the editors to rank a whole range of potential problems on a scale of one ("not a problem") through to five ("a major problem"). So here are the top ten reasons your idea might get turned down – and what you can do to try and ensure that it isn't.

Ten reasons editors turn down ideas

The first is that the idea is irrelevant to the newspaper, magazine, tv or radio programme or website to which it's sent. This is the top reason mentioned by editors (it scored 4.3 on our scale). The sad fact is that most of what pings into editors' in-boxes bears no relationship to the kind of topics that they want to cover. To give just one example, almost all the local newspaper editors we spoke to mentioned that they get lots of story offers which fall outside their circulation areas. Everybody should know that local newspapers are only interested in local stories, so it's a waste of time sending an idea which refers to something taking place 100 miles away. But it happens all the time. The remedy here is to find out what subject matter the publication is interested in and target offers more precisely.

The second worst problem the editors identified was that too many of the people who approached them had little idea of what their publication was like – and frequently hadn't even seen it. They ranked this as a 4.2 problem on the one to five scale. It stands to reason that you can't know whether a newspaper or magazine will be interested in what you have to offer unless you've actually seen it. It's not enough to rely on the title as a guide – a magazine may have the word "women" or "computer" in its title, but that doesn't mean it will be interested in everything to do with women or with computers. Newspapers and magazines differentiate themselves – and use their content to do so. The remedy here is to make sure that you have seen at least one recent copy of the newspaper or magazine before sending an idea to it. (The same principle applies if you are sending ideas to radio or television programmes or to new digital media, such as websites.)

The third problem was that many of the ideas offered to journalists were just too commercial or self-serving. This scored 4.1 on the scale. Journalists are looking for a good story or interesting information to include in a feature. They are not interested in writing what amounts to a free advertisement for the organisation offering the information. There needs to be something original and interesting that they can provide for their readers. So, the key question to ask yourself before offering information to the media is not: what can we get out of this? Instead, it should be: what have we got that we can offer that the journalist might want to know about?

And the fourth problem the editors identify is that the idea is relevant but that there is no "angle" – or a weak angle. This problem scores 3.5 on the scale. Most people have an inkling of what journalists mean when they talk about an "angle" on a "story". It means that the story has a new or unusual way of looking at the subject. But many of the ideas offered to journalists are little more than generalised requests to cover a particular topic or a block of background information about it. The ideas that succeed are the ones that tease out an original angle – something that, perhaps, the journalist hasn't thought about before.

Fifth in the list of problems – and with a score of 2.9 – was that the idea was a good one, but it was offered too late to get into the publication. Many people outside the world of newspapers and magazines have an unrealistic view of how late in their production cycle they take information and get it into print. Certainly, daily newspapers can take genuinely important information up to minutes before they go to press. But it's going to be exceedingly rare that you have information which fits into that kind of category. Often, even specialist journalists will be planning regular sections days, even a week or two, in advance. On monthly magazines, the planning cycle could begin anything from two to four months before the magazine is published. The time to get an idea accepted is when editors are planning their coverage rather than already working on what's going to be published.

The sixth reason why editors don't follow up on ideas sent to them is because they have the suspicion that the idea has been punted round to a lot of journalists at the same time. In other words, it's not exclusive. (Journalists rated this problem at 2.8 on their one to five scale.) Editors won't always want every story they run to be exclusive – that's not possible, anyway – but they are always looking for material that rivals haven't got. After all, it's by having unique coverage that they're able to differentiate their newspaper or magazine and make it attractive to readers. The way to overcome this problem is to make it clear when you're offering an idea that it is exclusive.

The seventh reason why an idea gets turned down is that the editor simply doesn't have the room to carry it. (This problem comes in at 2.4 on the scale.) Perhaps you're offering a long contributed article and the publication simply doesn't have the pagination to run it. Before sending in an idea, it's very important to check not only on whether the topic is relevant, but on the treatment of material the newspaper or magazine (or broadcast or digital media) runs. If you can match both subject matter and treatment, you could be on to a winner.

An eighth reason ideas get turned down (also 2.4 on the scale) is that the publication simply doesn't have the resources to follow up on it. This particularly applies when you're hoping that a reporter will come to cover your event. Over the years, many media – including top national media – have cut back on staff. That means more are looking for constructive help from PR people – but it often means they don't have resources for time-consuming follow-ups on story ideas. The answer is to present the idea in a way which minimises the amount of time that journalists need to get it into print or onto the airwaves.

Most journalists welcome constructive help from PR people, but sometimes PR people are not very reliable at delivering on the ideas they propose. When somebody gets a reputation for not being very reliable on bringing an idea to completion, journalists may start to doubt whether any of his or her ideas can make it into print. This is the ninth problem that the editors mentioned and they rated it at 2.2 on their scale. The solution is obviously to be certain that the idea can be delivered if the journalist wants to run with it.

Finally, the tenth problem the editors identified is that the idea is sent to the wrong person. Newspapers and magazines (as well as the broadcast media), apart from the smallest, have specialist editors and correspondents covering different subjects. It's important to check on who the right person is to contact before sending that e-mail or picking up the phone.

Of course, there is no guarantee that you will hit the spot with your idea, even if you studiously avoid all ten of these potential pitfalls. But they do represent 10 stepping steps to success – most of the time.

CHAPTER 3

BECOMING A SPOKESPERSON

Five reasons why it's important to put your case

Your time is valuable. Why spend it with journalists? Why not leave it to your public relations professionals who spend all their time dealing with the media? Isn't that what they're paid to do?

The fact is that any successful media campaign can only be successful when it is a partnership: between the public relations professionals – in-house or from consultancies – and other key figures in the organisation.

What do we mean by a "key figure"? From a journalist's perspective, it is somebody whose opinion they want when they write (or broadcast) about the organisation. In a company, that could well be the chairman or managing director. But it could also include a range of other directors and managers, depending on their function and their interest to the media. For example, experienced managers in specialised companies might be valuable sources of information for journalists working on niche publications.

But "key figures" don't only exist in companies. They also abound in the public sector and not-for-profit organisations, such as charities. At their most obvious, they include elected officials, such as MPs or local councillors. But senior civil servants, leading figures in executive agencies and top officers in local government could also find themselves facing journalists directly.

But it doesn't end there. There can be "key figures" in smaller organisations – often a source of information or comment for local newspapers and radio stations. In fact, these days the media has become so wide-ranging and pervasive that there are literally tens of thousands of people in all walks of life who might find themselves having to act as a spokesperson for their organisation. Naturally, they will operate at different levels – from the figures who habitually feature on national news programmes to those who deal mostly with local media. But some of the basic rules about being a good spokesperson apply at all levels.

Key figures need to be in the front-line of their organisation's public relations effort for one simple reason. Usually, journalists don't want to talk to anybody else. Because they are key figures – for whatever reason – they are the people whose views count. If you're one of these key people in an organisation you probably have little choice about becoming a spokesperson. When the media wants comment from your organisation – or in your area of expertise – it will be you they are coming to. Of course, spokespeople need the back-up from public relations professionals. And, indeed, on occasions, the PR people will also be spokespeople. But, in many cases, that is not enough. There are still many cases when key figures need to step into the front-line and put their organisation's messages across. We've summarised when key figures are important as spokespeople in checklist one.

Checklist 1: Five reasons key figures need to be spokespeople

The reasons why you should put your case direct to the media are:

- *Knowledge*: You know more about your organisation, or about your part of it (if it's large), than anyone else. Briefing an intermediary takes time you can ill afford – and no matter how good your briefing, the intermediary still won't understand the subject as well as you.

- *Authority*: You are a senior person. What you say has the ring of authority. What helps to give you that authority is your position in the organisation, the relevance of your experience and your expert knowledge.
- *Decision-maker*: You are a decision-maker – and you can explain the reasons for those decisions better than those who were not involved in taking them.
- *First-hand*: You are doing the job, facing the competition and meeting the people with whom your organisation habitually deals, perhaps customers or clients. You have first-hand knowledge of all the circumstances, within your organisation and outside it, that influence its decisions and policies.
- *Acceptable*: In many cases, you are the only acceptable spokesperson to the media. They don't want to interview PR people or junior staff.

Three key roles you must perform as a spokesperson

So, as a manager and company spokesperson, just what is your role? It can be summed up under three headings.

1 *It is to set policy*. Too frequently, public relations activities are not closely enough related to the organisation's vision, mission and objectives. In conjunction with other managers, including public relations professionals, your task is to make sure your organisation has a PR policy that matches your mission and objectives.

2 *It is to formulate the messages*. In conjunction with other managers and your public relations advisers, you need to decide what messages will help your company achieve its corporate objectives and how they are best put across. After all, as a spokesperson you will need to feel comfortable with those messages. They will be taken as, and should be, your messages.

3 *You need to lead your PR team over the top*. As we have seen, there is a limit to what public relations professionals can achieve without involvement from the "key figures" in an organisation. You must take your place in the front-line and talk to the media. In doing so, you will provide a focus for your organisation's public relations – and pave the way for the PR department's other activities. Remember that talking to journalists is the most effective way of communicating your messages to them and building a long-term understanding which is the foundation and a purpose of all good media campaigns.

Joining battle in the interview arena

Journalists – friends or foes? The answer is neither. They are professionals with a job to do – which may involve them writing about your organisation in situations which are either helpful or unhelpful to it.

Whichever is the case, you should treat journalists like any business contact. And, remember, they are also likely to respond like any external contact. There is no need to fawn or ingratiate yourself. But, conversely, you certainly shouldn't treat journalists like something the cat dragged in. Just adopt your usual good business manners.

What are journalists like? Hollywood got it wrong. There is no journalist stereotype of the hard drinker with a trench coat and trilby. In fact, journalists are in the business for a variety of motives. Some like the lifestyle, others have a passion for the subjects they write about. Some have ideals about seeking and publishing truth. Others treat it as a nine-to-five job. Over a period of time you're likely to meet many types.

In any specialised area of journalism, it is possible to meet writers who have an encyclopaedic knowledge of the subject. There are others, perhaps new to the business, who've barely mastered first principles. In quite a few cases, you will meet journalists who will need help in understanding the context of a story. As people, journalists are as broad a cross-section of humankind as the rest of the population. There is nothing special about them. But there are two qualities that all good journalists have in common. First, they are anxious to preserve their independence and integrity. Second, they are sensitive to being manipulated.

As you meet journalists in the arena of the interview, you should understand that you both approach from different directions. Appreciating the differences – which are set out in general terms in checklist two – will help you to understand the nature of your task as a spokesperson. Not all of the differences apply in all cases. You should focus on the points which you believe are most important in your case.

Checklist 2: Two perspectives: interviewee and interviewer

Interviewee	Interviewer
Doers	Observers
You're paid to take decisions.	They're paid to watch and write.
Long term	Short term
You plan ahead.	The horizon is the next deadline.
Subjective	Objective
Your life is entwined with your organisation.	They view your organisation as outsiders.

Enthusiastic
You have a passion for your
organisation and its activities.

Dispassionate
They have no emotional attach-
ment. They want a good story.

Rational
You run your organisation in
a rational and logical way.

Intuitive
A good journalist has a "nose"
for a story.

Diffused
You have many tasks
– talking to journalists is just
one preoccupation.

Focused
Writing a given story is the one
task in hand for the journalist
who is interviewing you.

Specialist
You may have studied a
specialist discipline – and
may know more about it than
anyone else.

Generalist
The writer may be a general
assignment reporter – and
even a specialist will not
match your knowledge.

Depth
You know about your
organisation and its areas of
activity in detail.

Breadth
The journalist sees many
organisations. His knowledge
may be a mile wide but an
inch deep.

Sensitive
You will be concerned about
the way your organisation
is described and the
interpretation others may put
on the words used.

Indifferent
The journalist writes the story
as he sees it without reference
to your feelings.

Responsible	**Independent**
You may work within a hierarchy, constrained by policies and procedures.	The journalist has editorial freedom – especially a specialist correspondent or freelance.
Means	**End**
For you a story is not an end in itself – it is a way of helping to achieve an objective.	For the journalist, the aim is to get a story into print or on the air.

Three kinds of interviews you have with journalists

In most cases, you will find that you are interviewed in broadly two kinds of situations – but there is a third, and more unwelcome, situation. The three are:

1 When you or your PR people have set up an interview with a journalist for a specific purpose. Let's call this the *proactive interview*.

2 When you are responding to requests for information from a journalist, either about a topic concerning your organisation or about a topic on which he/she thinks you might have useful information or views. Let's call this the *reactive interview*.

3 When you are responding to requests for information as a result of a train of events deeply affecting your company but significantly outside its control. Let's call this is the *crisis interview*. (Communicating in crisis is dealt with specifically in chapter nine.)

You should start by understanding the frameworks in which each of these kinds of interview takes place and these are set out in checklists three to five.

Checklist 3: 10 features of the proactive interview

The proactive interview:

- Takes place at your invitation
- On a subject of your choosing
- Normally in favourable circumstances
- Usually at your choice of location
- At a convenient time
- Often face-to-face
- With a friendly (or at least not overtly hostile) journalist
- Asking probing but not hostile questions
- For an article or programme that may not be too time critical
- BUT: The journalist may seek to "hijack" the opportunity to pursue another topic. ▪

Checklist 4: 10 features of the reactive interview

The reactive interview:

- Takes place at the journalist's request
- On a topic he or she raises
- In possibly unfavourable circumstances (but often not)
- At a place of his or her choosing
- Or (usually) over the telephone
- At a time that may not be convenient
- With a journalist motivated to pursue a story of his/her own choosing
- With questions that may be inconvenient or hostile
- For an article or programme that may be time critical
- BUT: You could score by aiding the journalist with a helpful message that is relevant to the story. ▪

Checklist 5: Nine features of a crisis interview

The crisis interview:

- Takes place at the journalist's insistence
- Under often unfavourable circumstances
- On the subject of the crisis
- About which you may not have full information
- In a situation that could be changing rapidly
- With questions that could be inconvenient, embarrassing or hostile
- For news media whose deadlines may be minutes away
- Or, in some cases, for live transmission
- BUT: By being prepared and remaining calm, you can show you are in control of the situation.

Exploiting the four forces that drive journalists

What makes journalists tick? They are professionals with a job to do and – as in most other kinds of business – the ones that get on are the ones that enjoy their work and do it best. Whether a journalist wants a full-scale interview or just a simple piece of information, you can score by helping the journalist to do his or her job better.

Let's look at four driving forces in journalists' lives and show how, by reacting intelligently to them, you can help the journalist and achieve better and more positive media coverage for your organisation.(Incidentally, they're not the only driving forces in journalists' lives, but they're common to most.)

1 *Serving audiences well.* Only one thing makes a commercially successful newspaper, magazine or internet site – readers. Or, in the case of radio and TV, listeners and viewers. We could call readers,

listeners or viewers the "audience". Without an audience there will be no sales revenue (if the publication is sold) and certainly little advertising revenue. Successful publications – and successful journalists – know instinctively what their readers want to read. The journalist's primary task is meeting the needs of readers, rather than helping you to put your message across.

This means that when you're planning to meet a journalist, you need to make sure you understand the content, treatment and style of the publication. Then you need to adapt your message to match those three main criteria:

- *Content* is about what's in the publication or on the radio or TV programme. In other words, the subject matter. For example, are there regular "departments" or columns in the publication dealing with specific topics?
- *Treatment* is about how that subject matter is dealt with. What level is it pitched at? For example, is it general or specialist? Purely factual or opinionated? Is it overlaid with the publication's or programme's point of view? Does it have lots of examples and quotes?
- *Style* is about how the material is presented. For example, are there lots of pictures, and if so what of? Does the publication use cartoons, graphs, technical drawings? Has the publication or programme been styled to appeal to a particular audience?

2 *Getting a good story.* Journalists don't actually shout "hold the front page", but a strong story, especially an exclusive, still makes the adrenaline pump faster. It's always difficult to interest journalists in a tired old piece of information. But it's never hard to interest them in a genuinely "good" story.

So if you have what you consider to be a "good" story – one that you're certain they will go for, and which serves your objectives

– consider carefully how to make the most of it. You need to market your story effectively. For example, there might be one main publication that covers the audience you want to reach. You might gain most coverage by giving the story to that one publication – the fact that the story is exclusive increases its value to that publication. Alternatively, there may be several publications – each with a different focus – that reach your audience. Tailor your story to each. And parcel the story up. Try to make sure that each publication gets a bit of exclusivity.

But a word of caution. In the long run, you must be seen by journalists to be fair and even-handed. Journalists can resent favouritism – especially when they're on the wrong end of it. In a market served by several rival publications, they all ought to receive fair treatment from you.

3 *Beating rivals.* Newspapers and magazines – and most radio and television stations – are commercial organisations like any other business and are in competition with one another. Journalists generally relish the competitive cut and thrust involved in beating rival publications to a story. And they are not just playing games – at worst, their jobs can be at stake.

There are times when you can turn this to your advantage. For instance, if you're known as a reliable and interesting source of comment about your industry, there could be times when you can help a newspaper scrambling to catch up with a rival that has got a story it missed by providing new facts, background information or informed comment.

That paper will be looking for a new angle or fresh material in order to take the story further – for example, by putting it in a broader context or perspective. Or it may be seeking to "rubbish" the rival's story. Being available and having something useful to say can put you into the news in a way that can be helpful to your organisation. It does not matter that the original story was not your own. The door may even have been opened by a competitor. But if you have information that can take the story further, or provide a better example, you can secure valuable coverage.

4 *Hitting deadlines.* Time is a tyrant for most of us. But in no industry is this more the case than in radio or television or in newspaper and (to a lesser extent) magazine publishing. When a story is breaking, a journalist needs information and comment fast – it could be in a matter of minutes. If you become known as a spokesperson who provides reliable information quickly, journalists will turn to you. And you could receive positive and helpful coverage for your company.

The converse is true. The biggest story since World War II that arrives after the presses have started to roll will not make it to the paper. (Although it might make it to the next edition, if it is a morning or evening paper with several editions.) But, in the case of the majority of trade newspapers or magazines that only have one edition, if it isn't a big story, it may be too stale to use by the next issue.

Taking all four points together, the key is that understanding what drives journalists, and being genuinely helpful – even when there doesn't seem to be any immediate publicity pay-off for you – will build a fund of goodwill that could eventually translate into more extensive and more positive coverage for your organisation.

How to find the best spokesperson

Who in your organisation would make the best spokesperson? Perhaps you need more than one spokesperson. In a large organisation with many divisions that will certainly be the case. But each spokesperson will need to have a blend of two kinds of qualities – relevant experience and a helpful personal attitude. Checklist six sets out in more detail the experience-based qualities needed by a spokesperson. Checklist seven sets out the personal qualities.

Checklist 6: Eight experienced-based qualities needed by spokespeople

Ideally, your spokesperson should:

- Understand and be committed to the vision, mission and strategy of the organisation and the key requirements for success.
- Have first-hand knowledge, at a senior level, of the organisation.
- Have a broadly based understanding of the organisation as a whole
- Have contributed to the formulation of the PR strategy that will support your organisation's mission and objectives.
- Have broad experience of the organisation in order to be able to take a balanced perspective.
- Be able to take an outward looking view of your organisation and the part it plays in its area of activity and society generally.
- Have the time to perform the duties of a spokesperson in addition to other work.
- Consider those duties as a key element of his/her responsibilities rather than just "something extra" to do. ■

Checklist 7: Seven personal qualities needed by spokespeople

Ideally, your spokesperson should:

- Be sensitive and responsive to the values, concerns and

interests of others
- Have a friendly, out-going personality
- Be articulate, but not verbose
- Have a good speaking voice (especially important for radio and TV)
- Be of smart appearance, and for TV at least, look fairly "normal"
- Have pleasant behaviour in social situations (for example, people who smoke insensitively, drink excessively or swear unrestrainedly can be an embarrassment)
- Have the enthusiasm to be a spokesperson.

Besides the formidable lists of qualities in checklists six and seven, it also helps if the spokesperson is as senior within the organisation as possible. It adds to his or her credibility. But it is not always the case that the most senior person makes the best spokesperson. However, there may be cases when only the top person will do. And if that is the case, he or she should try to develop all the qualities needed when called on to be a spokesperson.

Chapter 4

How to reach the people who matter

Finding the starting point for a communications campaign

Many communications and public relations campaigns fail to achieve their objectives. Too many. And they do so because they have not been planned and/or implemented with enough care. Activity – and there may be much of it – does not lead to the desired results. Everything you do in your organisation – almost everything, at any rate – should serve your organisation's mission and help it to achieve its objectives. This is what you are paid for and a communications campaign is no exception.

So just what is the starting point? Many organisations appreciate the value of positive media coverage and have gone out of their way to court it for many years. Others are more circumspect about media coverage. Some only realise that positive media coverage can help when their organisation faces a specific problem. If the organisation is a company that problem could be:

- Falling sales of a flag-ship product.
- Lack of awareness of new offerings.
- An inability to penetrate a new market.
- Difficulty in differentiating the company or a product from competitors.
- Failure to attract quality or specialised staff.
- Constraints on business success applied by governments or other public bodies.
- Loss of trust with an important group of stakeholders such as

investors or a local community.

- Risk to reputation because of the accusations, opposition and hostility of others.

If the organisation is a government department or some other kind of public authority, the trigger that makes people realise the organisation needs to raise its game could be:

- Public criticism of a new policy.
- Failure to get people to use a new service.
- Failure by the public to understand the benefits the organisation can deliver.
- Loss of trust with a section of the community that feels "excluded" or "ignored".
- Uncertainty caused by ministerial or other changes.
- Criticism in an official report or a disappointing position in published league tables.
- Adverse publicity resulting from a particular case.

If the organisation is a not-for-profit organisation, membership-based society or association, or a charity, the trigger that causes it to review its approach to media coverage could be:

- Low recognition of the organisation and its activities.
- Fall in membership.
- Drop in donations from charity appeals.
- Shortage of volunteers.
- Failure to influence public bodies in areas the organisation considers important.
- Government intervention in an area that was previously left to the voluntary sector.
- Failure of the government to consult.
- The activity with which the body is concerned appears to

become less fashionable.

• The body finds another occupational group encroaching on its space.

And, of course, there are many, many other triggers that could cause you to look at the effectiveness of your communications. The nature of the problems will reflect what your organisation does. As you can see, all these problems – and the many other examples that could be mentioned – have a specific focus. In almost all cases, the problem arises from failing to communicate effectively with specific groups of people – your audiences.

So the starting post is to decide which audiences you need to reach in order to achieve your objectives. We'll deal with that issue in this chapter. Then, in chapter five, we'll work out how to devise messages that can effectively reach your target audiences and serve your objectives.

But before you start to focus your mind on the audiences, you need to refresh your memory about your organisation's most important objectives. And you need to identify any specific problems where improved communication is needed. Finally, remember this key point: the purpose of effective media communication is to reach those audiences with messages that can help your organisation to fulfil its mission and achieve its objectives.

Two issues you must address to reach your target audiences

You have established that, in order to achieve your objectives or to overcome specific problems, you need to communicate effectively with your target audiences. Depending on the size of your organisation, that could be a lot of people in many different walks of life. Your time is valuable. You must use it effectively. And that means recognising you can't communicate with all of the people all of the time. So you need to identify those audiences that are most important – and target your messages at them. Those important audiences could include people both outside and inside your organisation.

In fact, you face two issues in seeking to reach your chosen audiences:

1 *You need to focus on the most important targets.* Don't believe that you can reach everyone. In any event, a message that is aimed at everyone is often of interest to no-one. Besides, no organisation needs to reach everyone. Remember, the people out there who might be interested in your message are only half listening. They don't sit around waiting for pearls of wisdom to drop from your lips. They've got other matters on their minds. If you say something that is half interesting to them, they might prick up their ears and take notice. But it must be of real interest – and, ideally, it must be aimed at them.

2 *You need to select the most effective channels for conveying your messages to these different audiences.* In most cases, you'll be reaching your audiences through third-party intermediaries – newspapers, magazines, radio and television programmes and, increasingly, websites. So you need to decide which are likely to be the most effective. (Incidentally, the fact that most channels are not directly controlled by you does not preclude you from creating your own, such as customer or staff newsletters or magazines and your own website.)

Defining the people you need to reach

So which groups of people do you need to reach? There is no one answer to this question as every organisation will have its own profile of potential audiences. Factors which affect decisions about audience include the scope and reach of your organisation. Checklists eight, nine and 10 are designed to get you thinking about potential audiences.

Checklist 8: 18 potential audiences for a company

- Management
- Staff
- Contractors
- Potential employees
- Sales team
- Suppliers
- Dealers/distributors
- Business partners
- Retailers
- Customers
- Potential customers
- Rivals' customers
- Non-users
- Local communities
- Government/public bodies
- Elected officials
- Investors
- Special interest groups.

Checklist 9: 12 potential audiences for a public body

- Residents in the areas served by the body
- Taxpayers
- Voters
- Employees

- Potential employees
- Contractors
- Users of the body's services
- Influencers and community leaders
- Suppliers of goods and services
- Other public bodies
- Service partners
- Advocacy/special interest groups. ▧

Checklist 10: 13 potential audiences for a charity, membership body, or not-for-profit organisation

- Beneficiaries
- Potential beneficiaries
- Donors
- Potential donors
- Members
- Potential members
- Government ministers
- MPs, MEPs, MSPs, AMs, peers
- Councillors
- Appointed members of relevant public bodies
- International bodies
- Companies
- Professional associations. ▧

Why not start by working through whichever of these three checklists is most relevant to your organisation and ranking each target audience's importance to your organisation on a scale of one to five – where one is most important and five least important.

(Of course, you might have target audiences not mentioned – it would be impossible to make the checklists comprehensive for every conceivable set of circumstances.) When you've done that you will have defined in general terms who your target audiences are. Depending on how precise you want to be in defining your audiences, you may want to write more specific descriptions of the kind of people you are seeking to reach. For example, if "rival's customers" are a key audience, you could define them further along these lines: "Existing users of small business accounting software" or "People who have bought a pair of tennis shoes in the last year". When you're going through this exercise, it is important that you should make your descriptions:

• broad enough to include all people who could be of interest to you in that category, but
• narrow enough to produce a clear focus and exclude people who really are of no or very small concern to you.

The more precise and selective you are in defining your target audiences, the more successful your communications are likely to be. You will be able to develop messages that most persuasively reach your target audiences and you will use your limited resources to best effect.

Using media channels to reach your target audiences

Now that you have decided on the people you most want to reach with your messages, the next task is to decide on the best means of reaching them. In other words, you need to identify the channels you will use.

If you are a UK organisation you have the whole British media to choose from. The whole overseas media, too, if you are concerned to project your message to foreign markets. But the key to success is selectivity. There are more than 11,000 regularly published newspapers, magazines and periodicals just in the UK. More than 200 radio stations, dozens of terrestrial, satellite and cable television stations. But you don't have unlimited time to devote to meeting the media. So priorities are important. Selection is essential.

You have three tasks:

1 You need to identify those newspapers, magazines, broadcast programmes and websites whose own audiences most closely match those you are seeking to reach.

2 You need to match your specific audiences to specific target publications. In other words, you need the right channel for each audience.

3 You need to introduce the human factor. To get the best results, you should identify the individuals – reporters or broadcasters – on your target media who are the people you need to reach. In the final analysis, it is people you have to talk to.

There are 15 main channels in which to locate the publications or programmes that will provide you with the best chances of reaching your audiences and checklist 11 provides brief details of them (using the UK as an example).

Checklist 11: 15 media channels

- International media. Includes newspapers with overseas circulations, specialist magazines with overseas circulations, CNN, etc and the World Service of the BBC.
- National newspapers. Includes daily and Sunday papers. Many of them run specialist sections on subjects ranging from computers to fashion, from business to gardening.

- Regional newspapers. Includes morning and evening papers. Always a strong regional bias, and with a special interest in organisations with a strong local base or activities.
- Local newspapers. Includes paid-for and freesheets (now a substantial section of the market). Total concern for local issues, including local business.
- Consumer magazines. The kinds of magazines you see on a newsagent's rack. Includes specialist magazines for women, leisure interests, sports, hobbies plus political and cultural activities.
- Business magazines. Includes some magazines on open distribution and some on subscription or controlled circulation. Includes general business publications with national or international circulations and regional business publications.
- Professional magazines. Includes publications aimed at specific professional groups, such as doctors, architects, accountants or solicitors. Sometimes produced in conjunction with a professional association.
- Trade and technical press. Mostly vertical market publications dealing with a specific industry or business area.
- Newsletters. Small circulation, specialist niche publications which often reach high-quality audiences in their chosen subject areas. Often circulated by e-mail.
- National television. Five terrestrial channels and now dozens of cable/satellite channels. Vast range of programming, but growing number of niche programmes which offer opportunities for organisations to provide material.
- Regional television. Regional ITV companies (now mostly under the centralised ownership), plus BBC regional services. Many produce own news and/or magazine programmes that

are interested in regional organisations.

- National radio. Five BBC and some commercial stations. BBC Radios 2, 4 and 5 Live, in particular, offer a range of specialist programmes with opportunities for coverage of a wide range of subjects.
- Local radio. More than 200 BBC and independent stations with a strong appetite for stories relating to their audience areas.
- Websites/e-newsletters. Increasingly important as a source of instant desktop reference in a wide range of industries and professions.
- Your own media. Newspapers, magazines, newsletters and websites designed and targeted to reach carefully selected internal or external audiences. Produced by your own organisation or specialist contractor. ■

The media described in checklist 11 are your potential channels of communication. You now need to match these channels to the different audiences you have already identified. This is a task which requires some care. In any sophisticated communications campaign, different messages will be aimed at different audiences. Some messages may be right for one audience, but not for another. You need to make sure that each message is satisfactorily targeted. And the best way to do that is to ensure that channels are carefully chosen.

You have now identified the main target media arenas where you want to concentrate your attack. But you need to be more precise. You need to match your specific audiences to the publications that will help you reach them. In order to do that, you need to get a clear idea of the individual publications or programmes in each of your priority media channels. You need to research – or get your PR professionals to research – the key channels (newspapers, magazines, radio and television programmes, websites) in each of your priority sectors.

There are a number of sources of information that can help you do this.

Sources of media targeting information

In fact, there are several commercial sources of information that can provide you with targeting information, but most of the sources have their advantages and disadvantages. They are:

Benn's Media. Benn's Media, first published in 1846, is probably the oldest media directory in the world. These days, it consists of an impressive set of four volumes containing listings of media. Volume one covers the United Kingdom, volume two the rest of Europe, volume three North America, and volume four most of the rest of the world. In all, the four volumes pack in 78,000 media entries with 187,500 named contacts in 214 countries. Obviously, the price changes from year to year but you could expect to pay around £200 for an individual volume or £400 for the lot. Benn's isn't a bad place to start if you want a low-cost and easy first port of call. The downside is that, like all printed directories, it is slightly out of date even by the time it is published and becomes progressively more out of date as time passes. Details from www. cmpdata.co.uk.

Willings Press Guide. This is in a similar league to Benn's and can be considered an alternative (or, possibly, even an addition), depending on how many reference books you want to accumulate. Willings Press Guide is also a long-established directory. It comes in three volumes covering, respectively, the UK, Western Europe and the World (excluding those countries covered in the first two volumes). The Guide provides information on 65,000 publications and media outlets which makes its range somewhat smaller than Benn's. However, unlike Benn's, there is also an online version, Willings Online, which is updated every three months. This makes searching easier and even lets you produce name and address labels in PDF format. Expect to pay in the region of £400 a year plus VAT for the guide and the online service. Details: www.romeike.com

Editors. Editors media directories have been around since 1982 and provide a very comprehensive listing of who's who and what's what in the British media. They also handily come in six compact volumes which means you don't find your arms yanked out of your sockets when you pick them up. Overall, there are 50,000 named editorial contacts on 15,000 publications and radio and television stations as well as specific programmes. But as with any printed directory, expect some of the names you're contacting to have moved on by the time you come to use the directory. Even so, if you're likely to want to use a wide range of media at different times, these directories could prove useful. Volume one (published monthly) covers national and Sunday papers together with news agencies and radio and TV. Volume two (quarterly) deals with business and professional publications, volume three (three times a year) with regional newspapers and tour guides, volume four (quarterly) with consumer and leisure magazines and volume five (three times a year) with television and radio programmes. Volume six (annual) is a useful round-up of freelancers together with members of the Writers' Guild (which represents writers in TV, film, radio, theatre, animation and books). Volume seven (published three times a year) is a guide to internet media. Expect to pay around £300 for annual subscriptions to individual volumes or around £700 for the lot. Details: www.romeike.com

PR Planner. If you want something a bit more sophisticated than a printed directory – even one that's updated online – you might want to consider *PR Planner* which has appeared for years on CD-Rom and is now out on DVD. It lets you search for publications and journalists on your PC screen and compile press lists which you can then print straight on to labels. Alternatively, you can produce e-mail or fax lists for distribution (but be aware that most journalists don't take kindly to you distributing your press releases on their paper). The disk contains 120,000 contacts in 49,000 organisations in the UK and the rest of Europe and it's updated every quarter so you can be reasonably certain you're working with contemporary information. Expect to pay around £900 plus VAT for the disk with the UK media information. Details: www.romeike.com

Mediadisk. By far the most comprehensive source of information – but also the most expensive – is Mediadisk. It is, essentially, an online database service with 700,000 contacts – a number that is larger than the population of 39 countries – in more than 165,000 media outlets around the world. This is clearly a service for the big user not least because it's the highest-tech of the services on offer. Romeike, which operates the service, says that Mediadisk receives about 2,000 updates a day which sounds good until you realise that means each of the 700,000 entries is only updated on average about once a year. Not all entries would need updating annually but some would need more frequent updates. Mediadisk has two helpful features. One is the ability to look up forward article plans on newspapers and magazines rather than trawling through other sources. The other is the ability to record activities and correspondence with individual journalists using the relationship management part of the system. But all this comes at a price.

Expect to pay around £3,200 plus VAT a year for a single-user licence. Details: www.romeike.com

In each of your essential target media channels you should draw up a short-list of several priority publications or broadcast programmes. Then you need to get more information on each of the names on your short-list before deciding on your final priorities. You can do this by studying each of your short-listed publication's media packs – the promotional material issued by the publication's advertising department – and sample issues. In the case of broadcast media, you need to study programme listings and view or listen to video or sound tapes of short-listed programmes. Ask yourself these questions:

- Do the short-listed media match the target audiences I have identified?
- Will the media be interested in the kind of information my organisation has to provide? Is our message relevant to the media's content?
- Are the treatment and style of the publication, programme or website likely to prove helpful in getting our message across to our end-audience?
- Is the media accessible: will it want to hear my message and is it likely to use it? Try to be completely objective about answering this question. Because people are naturally wrapped up with their own organisations, they often tend to over-estimate the amount of interest outsiders will show in it.

You need to have a fairly confident "yes" to each of those questions before you make any publication or programme a priority target for proactive attention.

When you have completed the exercise – and no-one is pretending it doesn't take time – you need to align your prime target publications and programmes with your audiences. At this stage, you are linking the people you're seeking to reach with the media – newspapers, magazines, programmes on radio and television, or websites – that they are likely to read, watch, listen to, or visit. This is a key part of your preparation, because you will want to know which messages to use in which media. When you've completed this exercise, ask two more questions:

- Am I satisfied with these priorities?
- Do they seem right for the needs of our company at the moment?

If you are not satisfied, make amendments. By the time you've completed this exercise, you should have ranked your most important audiences and identified the key channels through which you can reach them. But you've not quite finished. You still need to add those individual journalists or broadcasters within your preferred media who will be key to getting your message across.

How to make the human factor work in your favour

In any activity, the human factor is important and this is especially true of the world of media communications. So it helps to find out which media people are going to be most interested in your messages. You have already identified the target media which are the highest priorities in your pro-active public relations campaign. Now you need to target those writers or broadcasters – in the case of radio and television, often researchers – who will be most interested in your message. In many cases, this means identifying the specialist correspondents that might want to write about your organisation. There are three main ways to do this:

1 Refer to the specialist publications and media directories mentioned earlier.

2 Get copies of the publications on your preferred list. Study them carefully. See which journalists write about topics that might make them interested in your company.

3 Call the publication or programme and ask. Speak to the editor on smaller publications. On larger publications, generally ask for the news editor or features editor. In the case of radio or television programmes, the producer, editor or a researcher. Make notes of the names as you do this and keep accurate contact details up to date.

If you are interviewed by a journalist, it helps to know something about their special interests and the approach they take to writing about different subjects. Now that you have clearly identified your preferred publications and target journalists, you are in a position to get your PR staff to keep a cuttings file of the major pieces by your target journalists. In this way, you will develop a feel for the approach the journalist adopts when writing about your area of activity and the kinds of subjects he or she is interested in.

Remember, journalists are people and they identify with other people that seem to be on their wavelength. The human factor is as important between a journalist and the people he or she interviews as in any other business-like relationship – quite probably more important than in most. In the same way as any other business-like relationship, it works best when there is mutual respect and trust. Taking the trouble to understand a journalist's interests and approach will provide you with a significant edge in getting the journalist interested in your message and will be helpful if you meet for an interview.

You should now have a clear idea of the priorities of your audiences and of the pathways to them.

CHAPTER 5

CREATING MEMORABLE MESSAGES

Why effective messages are important

As a spokesperson, you are in the front-line when it comes to putting your organisation's case to the media. If you are to do this effectively you will, as we have already seen, be closely involved in relating your organisation's communications campaign to its mission, aims and objectives. But you will also need to play a significant role both in developing the kinds of messages that are put to the media and in putting those messages yourself in direct meetings with journalists.

But before we look at the detail of developing effective messages, it is useful to answer two important questions:

1 *What is a message?* As far as the media is concerned, a message is any information that it gets from your organisation. A well-thought out and carefully drafted statement is a message. So are hasty and ill-conceived remarks gabbled to a journalist over a telephone between meetings. "I haven't got time to talk to you" is a message. "No comment" is a message.

The lesson here is that if you want your organisation to be presented positively in the media, it needs to understand the importance of developing and delivering effective messages. The key word here is effective. Many organisations send out huge amounts of information to the media, but too little of it is effective communication. Like firing a blunderbuss, they spray out information indiscriminately. Some of it may score a hit, but much of it will be wasted. And some may even do unwanted damage. Because it was not properly targeted, it may be misunderstood and misinterpreted by its recipients.

In seeking to reach everyone, these organisations reach no-one. In wanting to say everything, they say nothing. They confuse rather than clarify. You need to make sure that does not happen in your organisation. As a spokesperson, you need to manage the communication process in your company so that only effective messages are communicated to the media. The modern phrase is "being on message".

And what does being on message mean? All activity should have a purpose. When you're on message, you're achieving more than merely telling people what you're doing. You are showing people what you're doing. And why. Being on message is all about promoting understanding to the audience which you're seeking to reach. In promoting understanding, you are helping to shape attitudes. And it is other people's attitudes - potential customers to your products, neighbours to your factory development plans, potential donors to your charity appeal, employees to your restructuring plans, users of your public services - that play a vital role in helping or hindering your organisation when it seeks to achieve its objectives. And that brings us to the second question.

2 *Why do we need messages?* As we have seen, an effective message is more than just a collection of facts and figures, or of bald unstructured information. It is designed to promote understanding, generally within a clearly defined audience of people. That means the information about anything you want to communicate - your organisation's annual report, the appointment of a new chairman, an important planning decision - has to be structured and shaped to generate that understanding. Information by itself does not

lead to understanding. Too much information, poorly structured information, badly targeted information can get in the way of understanding.

Having said that, it doesn't mean the information you want to provide has to be distorted. Still less, does it mean that it has to be artificially "manufactured". If your message is less than the truth, if it fails to be an effective representation of what you are trying to achieve, it will not ring true anyway. By structuring and shaping your message, we mean presenting the information you have to provide in a way that promotes the understanding you are hoping to generate. And hence shape attitudes in the way you want.

Moreover, when messages have been created, it is important that all people in the organisation who are acting as spokespeople - and who may have some responsibility for communicating them to the media - know and understand them. But a typical reaction from a person nominated to be a spokesperson and meet the media is this: "I know my organisation. I've been working for it for years. I'll have no difficulty talking about it and answering questions."

That casual approach to being a spokesperson usually ends with tears before bed time. That is because talking about your company to the media is not the same as chatting about it casually to friends in the pub. Time after time, when people fail to communicate what they want to say effectively or get into difficulty in interviews with the media, it is because they have adopted that kind of casual approach. They have not taken the time to prepare or understand their messages beforehand. It is precisely because you are so close to your organisation, subjectively involved in its activities and emotionally committed to its success, that you need to stand back and understand clearly those messages you want to put across to outside audiences – and the impact those messages are likely to have on them.

In most cases, when you meet journalists you are not being asked to talk generally about your organisation and its activities. You are being interviewed about a specific topic for an article with a focus that the journalist will create. If you are clear in your own mind about the messages you want to convey - and about the implications of those messages for your organisation - you will be able to deploy them more persuasively to your interviewer and influence the focus of his or her article or broadcast.

Three kinds of messages

As we saw in chapter two, there are three broad situations in which you might be interviewed – proactive, reactive and crisis. As a spokesperson for your organisation, you will need to provide messages to fit those three sets of circumstances:

1 *Proactive messages.* These are the messages that you want to convey about your own organisation, its aims and objectives and what it does. They are the positive statements that will help to fulfil your organisation's mission, achieve your objectives and shape the public's perception of your organisation as you want it to be seen.

2 *Reactive messages.* These are messages that you will be asked to provide by the media in reaction to things such as developments in your industry, the reaction of people to events, or some real or perceived failure on the part of your organisation.

3 *Crisis messages.* These are the messages that you will need to have ready in advance to deal with inevitable media interest in any major reverse, mishap or disaster that hits your organisation or in which your organisation has an interest.

Each of these types of message - proactive, reactive, crisis - could have a number of features. Before you start to draw up the specific messages for your organisation, it is useful to understand the different features that messages can have. If you know about these features, it will help you to understand more clearly the kind of message you are developing. And by doing that, you will be able to shape the message more precisely both to serve your organisation's own objectives, and to provide an effective communication through your targeted media to your ultimate audiences.

As a means of focusing attention, it is useful to consider the message features in four pairs. You will need to decide whether any or all of these pairs are relevant to the message you are developing. But if any are, it is worth considering the points they raise as you develop your message.

1 Is your message *strategic* or *tactical*? A strategic message is fundamental to your organisation's mission. It lies at the heart of what your organisation exists to do or promote. You should consider the message's impact on the different audiences it will reach. A tactical message aims to help you achieve a given objective or objectives. It is important for your operations but not central to your existence. You should consider whether the message has been targeted precisely enough to the audiences it is intended to reach.

2 Is it a *single* or a *multiple* message? A single message consists of just one central idea or theme. You should consider whether the message has been expressed with sufficient clarity to promote the understanding you seek. A multiple message consists of a cluster of ideas that inter-relate to one another. You should consider the danger of the media using only part of the message in the absence of the full context.

3 Is it an *exclusive* or *divisible* message? An exclusive message is aimed just at the one audience you are concerned to reach. You should consider the effect of the message reaching audiences other than those for which it is primarily intended. A divisible message

can be divided into its component parts and targeted at different types of audience. You should consider the effect of the message reaching audiences for which it was not primarily intended.

4 Is your message *good news* or *bad news*? Good news is, obviously, positive information that you are anxious should reach the widest possible audience. But you should consider the danger of hype making genuine good news seem "too good to be true". Bad news is, plainly, negative or unhelpful information that you cannot avoid releasing to the media or which they will learn about, in any event. You should consider ways of reducing the impact, including presenting the information in a positive context, or blunting its effect by coupling it to an item of good news.

Using proactive messages to help achieve your objectives

You now need to develop the specific proactive messages you are going to use to support your mission and objectives. You also need to be sure that your messages are going to support the image you want to portray.

So what kind of subjects can form the raw material for your messages? In chapter three, we looked at three sets of audiences you may want to reach with your messages. In checklists 12, 13 and 14, we look at some of the kinds of subjects you might consider for messages for each of the audiences. The checklists are not intended to be fully comprehensive. Indeed, in each category there could be dozens, if not hundreds of potential message areas. But they do show the kinds of areas that you might look at for suitable messages for given audiences.

Checklist 12: 15 company audience messages

- Company results
- Management changes and appointments
- Acquisitions and divestments
- Mergers and joint ventures
- New orders
- New investment
- New products
- New projects won or completed
- Opening of new premises or operations
- Inventions, discoveries or scientific breakthroughs
- Bonuses, awards and incentives
- New manufacturing processes
- Quality procedures and requirements
- Price and discount arrangements
- Advertising and other promotional campaigns.

Checklist 13: 12 public body audience messages

- New national or community services
- Changes of staff or officers, such as new mayor
- Improved sources of information
- Changes to opening hours, eligibility, etc
- Extra resources for services
- Efficiency savings or gains
- Number of people helped by services
- Examples of successful service delivery
- Position in league tables
- Ministerial or other visits
- Exchange arrangements, such as town twinning

• Career opportunities in public services. ▪

Checklist 14: 12 charity, membership body, not-for-profit audience messages

• New charity appeal
• Support of prominent backers or new patrons
• Amount raised from previous appeal
• How money raised was used
• Result of successful lobbying or representation
• New services for members
• Growth in membership
• Services delivered to targeted groups
• Examples of people helped
• Changes of staff
• Election/appointment of new officers
• Awards/commendations received. ▪

As you can see from these three checklists, there is a huge number of possible messages for target audiences and a vast number of possible combinations of messages and audiences. You need to prioritise. Because there could be such a huge number of potential messages, you need to select the possible messages that will most effectively reach your priority audiences and help you to achieve your specific objectives.

As you do this, be specific, not vague. If you want to gain immediate practical benefit from this exercise you should look for subjects that you could use during the next six months.

By going through the admittedly rigorous task of listing, defining and prioritising the messages you could disseminate over the next few months, you will have effectively drawn up an agenda for action. Moreover, you will have created a situation in which the information you do disseminate to the media should both serve your immediate objectives and create better understanding of your organisation and its activities among your priority audiences.

But just as your immediate objectives may change rapidly within the overall framework of your organisation's mission and aims, so might your specific messages. For this reason, you need to identify and prioritise messages regularly. Remember that in any dynamic organisation, specific messages may change quite rapidly. For that reason, you ought to undertake this exercise once or twice a year, or whenever required by significant developments and particular events.

How to develop reactive messages that work

No organisation operates in a vacuum. It carries on its activities in a world in which a myriad different influences could be acting upon it. Those influences could include the government and public bodies, other businesses and organisations, the local community as well as special interest and advocacy groups.

This means that, as a spokesperson, you will sometimes be called upon to comment on events that are taking place in the wider world. You might consider this an unwelcome interruption to your daily life. Or you might think that it obscures the main thrust of your proactive media messages. In fact, if you do three things, you can make your reactive messages as effective in serving your mission and objectives as your proactive messages. These three things are:

1 *Anticipate.* With careful and intelligent thought you can identify those areas where you could be called on to provide

a reactive message. Often that message would be as a result of something that a third party has done or is planning to do. Third parties whose activities may be relevant to your organisation are listed in checklist 15.

Checklist 15: 17 types of bodies that could have an impact on your organisation

- Government: Which policies are likely to impact on your organisation?
- Parliament: Which new laws could impact on your organisation?
- Local councils/communities: Which local authorities could impact on your organisation? Which local pressure groups/individuals?
- European Union: Which legislation and directives could impact on your organisation?
- Foreign governments: Does your organisation have dealings in other countries whose governments could have an impact on it?
- Competitive organisations: How could their plans impact your own?
- Collaborative organisations: Which organisations/companies are you involved in joint ventures with (if any)?
- Professional/regulatory bodies: How will their rules and regulations impact on your organisation?
- Industry associations: How will their policies and view of your industry affect your business or organisation?
- Special interest/advocacy groups: How will the policies and activities of pressure groups impact on your organisation?

- Customers: How will the actions of important or high-profile customers affect your organisation?
- Investors: What actions of which major investors could impact on your organisation? Could you be a take-over target? From whom?
- Trades unions: Which unions are active or could be active in your organisation?
- Suppliers: Which companies supply your organisation with important goods, materials or components?
- Distributors/retailers: Which companies distributing or selling your products could have a measurable impact on your business?
- Terrorists/criminal gangs: Does your organisation have activities, operations, locations or processes that are at particular risk?
- Courts/tribunals/investigations: Are any cases or investigations likely or outstanding? █

Taking the different kinds of bodies and groups in this checklist, make a list of those bodies that are likely to have a significant impact on your organisation. Be specific as you do this. For example, don't just put "government", but list the departments or bodies that will specifically impact your organisation. Of course, just because a third party can have an influence on your organisation doesn't mean that it necessarily will do. Or that, even if it does, you will be called on to provide a reactive message. That depends on other factors.

So you need to relate the third parties that could trigger a need for a reactive message to your priority audiences. This will give you a correlation between the audiences you are seeking to reach and the possible reactive messages you might have to provide. When you have completed this exercise, you may find that there are only a limited number of high-ranking third parties that are likely to trigger the need for reactive messages. Given that this is a time-consuming exercise, you will be wise to limit yourself to those that are of the highest priority.

2 *Plan*. You have identified those areas in which you could be called on to deliver re-active messages. Now you need to work out how you are going to keep yourself informed about the relevant activities of those bodies you have marked as priorities to watch. You need to make sure that relevant activities of those third parties are monitored within your organisation. That is, potentially, a large task – for example, for a FTSE100 company, a large government department or agency, or a major charity it could be a huge task. But for smaller to medium-sized organisations, the job can be kept manageable by concentrating only on the priority areas you have identified. Checklist 16 sets out some of the sources of information that might be helpful.

> ## Checklist 16: 20 sources of information about organisations you need to know about

Sources of information about the third parties, whose activities you may need to monitor, include:
- Government websites and reports
- Parliamentary reports and proceedings
- European Commission documents and website
- European Parliament website, reports and proceedings
- Embassy websites/press announcements for relevant countries
- Minutes/websites of public bodies

- Company websites, reports, press releases
- Press cuttings services
- Special interest websites
- Reports/other documents from special interest groups
- Surveys/reports from "think tanks" or universities
- Market research data
- Analysts' reports (analysts cover most major industries)
- Industry association websites/reports
- Regulatory bodies' websites/reports
- Agendas, timetables and case lists
- Credit reports/agencies and Companies House
- Search engines such as Google
- Trade and other directories and reference books
- Professional/specialist advisers/newsletters. ▣

The checklist cannot hope to include every possible type of material that you could possibly want to monitor. But it will give you some ideas on where to search for it.

You need to make arrangements to monitor or receive regularly material that is likely to be relevant to your organisation. Then you need to set up a system to ensure the material is reviewed regularly and that all spokespeople are informed about information which bears on areas where they may need to develop reactive messages.

Depending on your other responsibilities in your organisation, you may choose to review the material yourself. Alternatively, you may choose to have it reviewed by someone else - a public relations or public affairs adviser, for instance - who will prepare a report, drawing your attention to key issues.

If you adopt this approach, it will not guarantee that you will never be caught out, but it will ensure that you develop a much deeper knowledge about how your organisation is affected by the world around it. It will also enable you to enhance your role as a spokesperson by becoming more knowledgeable about specific issues of importance to your organisation. The object of planning is to make sure that you are already informed and have had time to consider your response when called on to provide a message about an external event which affects your organisation or in which it has a legitimate interest.

Some organisations have a formal issue monitoring and management process. They track and prioritise significant trends and developments in the business and market environment – whether economic, political, social, environmental, technological and so on. They make a periodic assessment of their likely impacts upon the organisation and what action (if any) they need to take at local or head office level in response. There may be both challenges to address and opportunities to pursue. Find out if your organisation undertakes such an exercise – or an annual SWOT (strengths, weaknesses, opportunities and threats) analysis – and think about how you can plug into the findings and best use the results.

3 *Respond.* You have identified priority areas in which you may be called on to deliver a reactive message. You have taken steps to keep yourself informed about them. Now how should you prepare yourself for possible approaches from the media?

You need to be prepared with reactive messages which demonstrate to the media that you are knowledgeable and authoritative about the issues raised and that you have something distinctive and worthwhile to say about these issues. At the same time, you need to make sure that what you do say serves your organisation's objectives by enhancing its image and reputation with priority audiences. In most cases, if you have anticipated intelligently and armed yourself with relevant information, it is not difficult to make a reasonable assessment of what questions you could be asked. Make sure that when an issue arises that could result in a need for reactive comments you develop possible responses. Then check your planned response against the effective reactive message criteria in checklist 17.

Checklist 17: 10 effective reactive message criteria

- Has our message been checked against the four pairs of message features described earlier in this chapter?
- Does the message say something distinctive and worthwhile?
- Is the message credible?
- Are the facts supporting it completely accurate?
- Does the message support our organisation's objectives?
- Which media are likely to want a comment on this issue?
- Is our message likely to be of relevance to their special concerns?
- Have we identified any likely supplementary questions?
- Could the message be construed as in conflict with, or contradicting, other recent messages?
- Are there any unfavourable associations – for example, could our message be placed in an unhelpful context? ▩

Finally, you need to consider whether, in fact, this is an issue of sufficient importance to your organisation that it should become a proactive message. In other words, perhaps you shouldn't wait to be asked before you communicate your views. Above all, if you think there is a likelihood of your being asked to provide a comment about a developing issue or event, do not wait until you are asked. Prepare in advance - and you will be more effective.

(We have dealt with proactive and reactive messages, which leaves crisis messages. There are many special factors affecting crisis messages, and these are dealt with separately in chapter nine.)

How to create messages that grab media attention

So far you have identified what your messages should be about. Now you need to build and focus those messages so that they will be effective when you meet the media. So what are the features or characteristics of an effective media message? Checklist 18 sets them out in note form.

Checklist 18: 12 features of effective media messages

- Short: media people are busy. They don't have time to waste while you get to the point.
- Simple: a good message is easy to grasp - even by someone who is not an expert in your organisation's areas of activity.
- Specific: don't be vague. Make it clear what your message is about.
- Focused: the message should be developed with its ultimate audience clearly in mind.
- Tailored: it should also be crafted to meet the needs of the particular journalist or journalists who will be receiving it.
- Positive: in the words of the song, accentuate the positive, eliminate the negative.
- Accurate: a good message gets it right.
- Authoritative: it has the ring of credibility because it comes from a spokesperson who has the authority to speak and who

is in complete command of the subject.

- Appropriate: it's the right message in the right place at the right time.
- Jargon free: don't make it sound as if your message is in code.
- Distinctive: make sure your message is different. It should "add value" to the topic under consideration.
- Compelling: it should convince, appear definitive and be watertight.

Always remember that a message can usually be improved. The key tests in checklist 18 can help to focus on any areas of weakness in your message so that you can correct them. If your message has all the qualities listed in the checklist, it is well on its way to being the kind of message that will penetrate your target media.

Passing the so-what? test

A message could have all those qualities and still lack the two essential ingredients to make journalists sit up and take notice.

Is it *newsworthy*?

Is it *interesting*?

In other words, does it pass a key test that journalists often use when deciding whether to publish a certain item of information. It is called: *the so-what? test*. If the media failed to carry your message would their readers or viewers be any the poorer? Would they have been deprived of an important or useful piece of information? So how can you make sure that your message has all the qualities in the checklist and also passes the so-what test?

When you have drafted a message or piece of information for the media, it is useful to submit it to rigorous questioning. Checklist 19 sets out a number of questions in groups that you can ask as you seek to make sure that your messages pass the so-what? test.

Checklist 19: seven ways to make media messages pass the so-what? test

First:
- Have you really focused sharply enough on your audience?
- Have you identified with their needs?
- Do you understand their problems and point of view?
- Is your message really tuned into what they want to know?
- What – if anything - might the message cause them do differently?

Second:
- Is your message as simple as you can make it without distorting the meaning?
- Are you sure you can't refine it further?
- Have you really got to the heart of what you want to say?

Third:
- Does your message touch on newsworthy themes in your organisation or area of activity?
- Is your message plugged into the broader world?
- Have you shown an appreciation of the wider context in which you are making your message?

Fourth:
- Are you presenting your message clearly?
- Are you sure other people, without your special knowledge, can really understand it?

- From the way you have presented it, will they derive the lessons you want them to?

Fifth:
- Have you pitched your message at the right level?
- Are you sure you're not talking down to your audience?
- At the same time, are you certain you're not blinding them with science?

Sixth:
- Is your message supported with convincing facts, examples, case studies and other evidence?
- Does the supporting evidence effectively reinforce your message?
- In fact, is there a sufficient weight of supporting evidence to make your case convincing?

Seventh:
- Have you expressed your message as memorably as you can?
- Have you chosen your words carefully so that you light up rather than obscure your meaning?
- Have you avoided jargon and bureaucratic waffle?

So many organisations fail to get their messages across because they don't pay enough attention to refining them so that they will grab the media's attention. Return to your message and test it against the questions in checklist 19. See if you can construct your message in such a way that it meets your organisation's objectives, but at the same time fulfils the tests needed to make it pass the so-what? test.

If you have done so, you have almost certainly constructed a newsworthy message that will be effective with the media, enhance your organisation's desired image and fulfil its objectives.

Making sure the basics are in place

As a spokesperson, you will speak to the media about a wide range of your organisation's activities. The focus of individual messages you are called on to give will change from time to time. But there are certain questions you'll be asked repeatedly. Although these questions are not hard to foresee, it is surprising how many spokespeople are not able to answer them convincingly.

For example, if you work in a company, you ought to have the company's basic trading data at your fingertips – its market capitalisation (if it's a public company), turnover, last year's profit, number of employees, number of branches and so on. The exact range of statistics will vary from company to company depending on its size and the nature of its business. If you're working in a public authority, government agency, charity or non-profit making organisation, there will be other kinds of basic facts and figures which you ought to have readily to hand.

But beyond these basics, there are other features of your organisation that you ought to think about so that, if they come up in an interview, you have already developed messages to use in answering the questions. Many of these features cluster round what we can loosely call your organisation's image. As we have already noted, a spokesperson sets out to be more than a provider of information. You are trying to create understanding. Being able to talk fluently about these image issues will do much to help other people understand what makes your organisation tick and what it is trying to achieve.

To talk convincingly, you need to have a thorough understanding of all the elements that go to make up your organisation's image. And then you should use that understanding to work out ways of describing each of the elements of your organisation's activities in not more than three or four sentences. Those sentences ought to contain all the information the listener needs in order to understand the point you want to make. Whatever the actual subject matter of specific messages, you will constantly return to central issues about your organisation's corporate personality. These need to be woven skilfully into all your messages in order to build the image and understanding you are seeking to achieve.

Checklist 20 is designed to help you focus on some of the issues you need to address when developing those key messages that will help to shape your image. Involve your colleagues in discussing what your messages ought to be on these issues. Test your messages on people inside your organisation and on outsiders. Involve your public relations and public affairs advisers.

Checklist 20: 14 key issues when developing an image for your organisation

- Mission: What is your organisation's mission? What is its purpose?
- History: When was your organisation founded? What have been the significant milestones in its progress?
- Culture: What is your organisation's style? What is its philosophy in approaching what it does?
- Nationality: In which country did your company have its origins? Does it want to be known as a national or international company?

- Locations: How important is the location in emphasising the organisation's skills and expertise?
- Governance: How is your organisation controlled and managed?
- Organisation: How does your organisational structure contribute to its effectiveness?
- People: Who are the main people in your organisation? What do they bring to it?
- Markets/audiences: Which markets or audiences is your organisation aiming at? How is it being effective with those markets/audiences?
- Products and services: If a commercial organisation, what kinds of businesses are you in? What is the main focus of your products and services?
- Technology: Do you have a reputation for using technology effectively, perhaps to make you more accessible? What part does technology play in the organisation's success?
- Competition: Who are your main competitors? And why are you more than a match for them?
- Strengths and weaknesses: What are your organisation's strengths? And what have you to say about other people's claims about your perceived weaknesses?
- Differentiators: What is unique special or different about your organisation in the above areas and/or in its ways of working, relationships, terms of business, and so on. ▪

You have now spent a lot of time preparing your messages. The next step is to work out how you can present those messages so that the media sit up and take notice of what you have to say.

Chapter 6

Great preparation, great performance

Three things you must know before you face a journalist

Before you face a journalist, there are a few important things that it is desirable to know. It pays to take the time to find out about them – if necessary with the help of your public relations advisers. The things you need to know fall into three main categories: your interviewer, the purpose of the interview, and your organisation and message. We'll now examine each of those areas in more detail.

What you should know about your interviewer

As with any business meeting, it pays to know something about the person or people you'll be meeting before you do so. It makes the ice-breaking a little less painful when you meet. It helps you to tune into their wavelength more quickly. And, let's be honest, it gives you a psychological boost knowing you've got "something" on them.

Of course, it is not always practical to know much – or anything – about the journalists you'll be meeting. At a press conference with 50 news hounds, you can't know them all, let alone their life histories. But there are four circumstances, when you really must take the time to brief yourself. These are:

1 When you're facing a one-to-one interview.

2 When you're holding a small briefing for a handful of journalists (say not more than four or five).

3 When you're going on a facility trip with a similarly small

group of journalists.

4 When there is a handful of journalists who cover your industry or company and you're likely to meet them regularly at industry events or receive out-of-the-blue telephone calls from them for comments and quotes.

Your public relations professionals should be able to help with the spadework of finding out about these journalists. The kind of information you might want to know is set out in checklist 21.

Checklist 21: seven facts you must know about key journalists

- What is his/her correct first and second name? (Do you have them spelt correctly? How do you pronounce them, if tricky?)
- Which publications do they work for? (Have you ever seen a copy of them?)
- What position does he/she hold? (Is your information up to date? Have you missed a key promotion?)
- Likely knowledge/experience of your field of activity/ organisation? (A lot of background knowledge? Or will you have to get back to basics?)
- Any known special interests/"hobby horses"? (If so, do they support or conflict with your organisation's objectives and messages?)
- Any previous contact with your organisation? (What do they already know about the organisation? Whom have they met within your organisation?)
- Has he/she previously written about your organisation? (Was it sympathetic? Hostile? Neutral?) ◼

What you should know about the purpose of the interview

In some cases, you will have initiated the interview – it will be a proactive interview – but in others the request for the interview may come from the journalist. In these cases, it is essential to find out from the journalist what the purpose and focus of the interview will be. There could be a number of different reasons why a journalist wants to interview you and these are set out in checklist 22.

Checklist 22: seven reasons why journalists want interviews

- To pursue a specific hard news story or feature article. The focus is clear. It is about a specific product or project with which your organisation is involved, or about some development in the organisation itself.

- To increase general understanding. The focus is fuzzy. It is about building background knowledge of your organisation or area of activity.

- To obtain an example for a planned feature. The focus is specific. It is about finding relevant examples for a specific article.

- To seek information for a background article. The focus is clear but broad. The journalist may want "educating" on a topic about which he/she knows little.

- To seek evidence to support a point of view. The focus is clear but may be unhelpful if you do not subscribe to the point of view the journalist will pursue in the article.

- To obtain information on customers, clients or members. The true focus of the interview may be hidden. The journalist may not be primarily seeking information about your company, but about a customer/member in which he/she is particularly interested.

- To check out rumours, gossip, innuendoes, allegations of differences or other matters picked up on the grapevine or in bars. The journalist may sense a latent story, even a "cover up", but wants to "get a foot in the door" and "sniff around a bit" before judging whether or not a story exists.

In practically all cases, a journalist will be prepared to reveal the purpose of the interview in advance. And if he or she is not prepared to do so, it should certainly set some alarm bells ringing. If you know about the purpose of the interview in advance, you will be able to anticipate more easily the line of questioning and this knowledge will help you to prepare to present your messages in a way that both reinforces the corporate personality you are seeking to promote and is helpful to the journalist.

What you should know about your organisation and messages
As a start, you should be certain you have all the background information about your company – the kind of information that is too often overlooked – at your fingertips. We covered this is chapter four. In particular, refresh your memory on checklist 17 which shows you how to make sure the messages you plan to use in your interview will pass the "so-what?" test. You also need to be certain you are completely up-to-date on your organisation's activities in whatever areas will be discussed.

And you should try to anticipate the main areas that your interviewer is likely to want to know about and possible questions that may be asked. Remember that an interviewer will often want to probe behind the information you provide. When you volunteer information in an interview, have you thought about the likely supplementary questions it may provoke?

It is not advisable to try and prepare answers to all the questions that could be asked. That would probably be impossible, and in any event would lead to a stilted and possibly unproductive interview for both parties. But you should arrange to be well briefed on all the main areas that are likely to be discussed. And it is probably helpful to prepare a form of words to use in answer to questions about any especially sensitive areas. But you should avoid giving the appearance of parroting some kind of official line. And you will usually create a better impression by not reading from a prepared statement on a particular subject.

Finally, you need to make certain you have assembled everything you are likely to need during the interview before it starts. It gives an unprepared and unprofessional appearance not to have material to hand that an interviewer could reasonably expect that you would have. And it also wastes time and interrupts the flow of the interview if you have to search for material in the middle of it.

Checklist 23 suggests material that you may want to have to hand. But make sure you provide the information the journalist really needs rather than a ton of irrelevant bumph.

Checklist 23: 12 kinds of information a journalist may need at an interview

- Organisation backgrounder
- Relevant policy, organisation's value, mission statements, etc
- Product/service backgrounders
- Annual report and accounts
- Product/service literature
- Case studies

- Statistics/basic facts about the organisation
- Photographs
- Diagrams/charts
- Manager/interviewee biographies
- Relevant quotes
- Names of product users/dealers/etc for further contact.

Situations in which you will face the media

As a company spokesperson, you could meet the media in many different kinds of situations – some foreseeable, some unforeseeable. Some welcome, others less so. There are, of course, many features which apply in all situations. We have looked at those already. But there are also special features which apply in different situations. And being aware of the opportunities and problems in each different kind of situation will make you more effective as a spokesperson.

The main situations in which you'll meet the media, together with the opportunities and problems which they present, are described in checklists 24 to 34. Be particularly careful in all situations not to discuss matters under official investigation or before a court, or reveal confidential, or – if the company is quoted – "insider" or "price sensitive" information.

Checklist 24: opportunities and problems in a face-to-face interview

- When it happens: when you set up an interview with a journalist or respond to a request for interview.
- Opportunities: personal contact gives you the chance to put across your message most persuasively. There's nothing like

talking to people for effective communication. Meeting a journalist gives you the chance to develop a professional relationship as a springboard for future positive coverage.

- Problems: the interview could well be lengthy, probing and require detailed responses to questions. Personal like or dislike of the interviewer could colour your response and make your answers too effusive or too reticent.

Checklist 25: opportunities and problems in a telephone interview

- When it happens: generally at short notice from a journalist who wants a speedy response to a question or issue.
- Opportunities: gives you the chance to be seen in a positive and responsive light. Frequently provides an opportunity to plug into a story idea a journalist has developed and mould the idea with a message that serves your business objectives.
- Problems: a real risk of being caught wrong-footed on an issue you haven't given proper consideration to. The context of the journalist's story may not be helpful to the message you want to provide. Hasty off-the-cuff comments can give an impression you didn't intend to reveal or facts you would have preferred to remain confidential.

Checklist 26: opportunities and problems in a conference call interview

- When it happens: when several people want to join an interview from the same or different locations.
- Opportunities: gives you the chance to provide a broader range of comment and experience in an interview. Several

participants can add their own unique expertise which may give an interview extra depth and value for the journalist.

• Problems: practical differences sometimes arise with sound quality when people are in the same room and using a speaker phone. The interview may become confusing for the journalist if too many people are chipping in with different ideas in an unstructured way. The journalist needs to be able to recognise different voices so that quotes can be attributed accurately. Try to control the number of participants, as all of them may need to be carefully prepared, and the weakest member could let down the team. ▪

Checklist 27: opportunities and problems in an e-mail interview

• When it happens: when the individual the journalist wants to interview is not available to speak face-to-face or over the telephone, perhaps because of work commitments or time differences.

• Opportunities: provides a chance to think about e-mailed questions before responding to them in a considered way. Repeated requests for more information in extra e-mails can be handled in a more considered manner than a voice interview because there is time to think and/or research information. A good way to get a helpful quote into a journalist's story when there is no chance of an interview taking place.

• Problems: answers to questions can be too stilted and formal to be of much interest to the journalist. Alternatively, if the e-mailed questions are treated too casually, the answers may give away more than desired. Lack of personal contact may make it harder to "read between the lines" of the journalist's questions. Hastily prepared e-mails can come back to haunt. Remember that simply sending your e-mail is effectively "publishing your attributed comments to the world". ▪

Checklist 28: opportunities and problems at a press conference

- When it happens: usually to make a major announcement or to react to widespread calls from the media for a statement or comment about a particular situation.
- Opportunities: gives you the chance to prepare and present a message to a wide group of journalists at the same time. Enables you to present a key individual or team of people at first hand or use audio-visual aids to put across your message. The status of the event can improve coverage when properly used for major announcements.
- Problems: poor answers to unexpected questions can display a weakness in your case to a lot of journalists at the same time – which underlines the importance of careful preparation. Think carefully about who to include, as both journalists and colleagues may take umbrage if they are not invited. ▪

Checklist 29: opportunities and problems at a press briefing

- When it happens: at your instigation, normally to make an announcement that is likely to be of interest to a small group of journalists, or to provide background or insight to a development you want publicised, or to take the sting out of some item of negative news affecting your organisation by providing a broader and more positive context.

- Opportunities: gives you the chance to meet a small group of journalists which you select on your terms, sometimes on ground rules you will have defined. Provides the chance to give each journalist a personal face-to-face briefing in sufficient detail to promote the understanding you want to engender. Helps to establish personal relationships with journalists that can be of value in the future.

- Problems: journalists interested in a briefing would be likely to be well informed about your area of activity and/or organisation and could ask searching and possibly awkward questions. Because a very select event is more desirable for key journalists that attend, numbers will need to be kept low, which increases the risk that some other journalists might feel "excluded" and slighted. ▪

Checklist 30: opportunities and problems on a facility trip or visit

- When it happens: to show off your factory, office or other facility, or to visit sites of satisfied customers.

- Opportunities: provides the chance to show selected journalists the positive side of your organisation and its activities over an extended period of time, rarely less than a whole day. Shows journalists at first hand what you want them to understand – always more effective than telling them in a remote office. (Showing is always more effective than telling.) Gives you the chance to build positive working relationships with journalists you may not have previously known, or only know slightly.

- Problems: inadequate preparation can highlight weaknesses rather than strengths. Even with preparation, customers – if it is a customer visit – may not always say just what you'd like them to. Poor travelling arrangements and time wasting irritates journalists. ▨

Checklist 31: opportunities and problems at an exhibition

- When it happens: whenever you take a stand at an exhibition or organise your own.
- Opportunities: a chance to meet journalists interested in your area of expertise who might otherwise be difficult to get hold of. A chance to show your products and services, or showcase your activities, to journalists on your own terms.
- Problems: inadequate arrangements to meet or receive journalists on stands could lead to missed opportunities – or even create bad feeling. Not all staff chosen to deal with the general public on exhibition stands are ideal for discussing your organisation and its activities with journalists. You should consider whether those likely to meet journalists should be trained as spokespeople. Inexperienced staff could make comments or provide information to journalists that is not helpful to your organisation. ▨

Checklist 32: opportunities and problems at an annual general meeting

- When it happens: once a year in every organisation that is obliged to hold them. In the commercial sector, only the larger publicly quoted companies will normally attract press, especially if there is some chance of controversy or "bad" news. The latter might be more likely at a special general meeting, held when required/requisitioned.

- Opportunities: provides an authoritative platform for making statements about a organisation's past successes and future direction. The organisation's top decision-makers have the chance to explain policy and plans in an authoritative gathering. Provides a chance for the organisation to address, through the media, the mass of its shareholders or members not at the meeting.
- Problems: gives the chance for disgruntled shareholders or members to meet and put their grievances to journalists. The company's top people could be "ambushed" by journalists for off-the-cuff comments before or after the meeting. ■

Checklist 33: opportunities and problems at a conference or seminar

- When it happens: when you or other managers are invited to address a professional or trade gathering or other event.
- Opportunities: apart from speaking to those present, a speech delivered to an important industry, professional or other event can be of interest to the press. Regular speakers at conferences and seminars take on a special aura as "pundits" or "gurus" in the eyes of the press and become more "newsworthy".
- Problems: unguarded comments at conferences – especially in answer to questions – can be reported if journalists are present. Remember, the nature of the audience will be determined by the event organiser. It may be wise to arrange a briefing for colleagues who either speak, or are likely to speak, at public events as, in addition to journalists, key customers, competitors and other interested parties may also be present. ■

Checklist 34: opportunities and problems during door-stepping

- When it happens: rarely, and often in response to an event of major and newsworthy significance, often a crisis. Door stepping refers to journalists waiting outside someone's home or office or waiting for them to come off a plane or train so that they can be asked (direct and often hostile) questions.

- Opportunities: by remaining cool, calm and collected, the chance to show you are in control of the situation. By being pleasant in trying circumstances, the chance to win personal sympathy for your plight from the public.

- Problems: appearing flustered by the unwanted attentions of journalists, especially in television coverage, can give the appearance that you are not in command. Throw-away lines in response to shouted questions rarely put your case effectively and can give a grossly misleading impression. Displaying hostility to door-stepping journalists may present you in an extremely unfavourable light, especially on television, and may lose any residual sympathy for you among the journalists themselves.

So you've prepared thoroughly for many different situations. The next step is to discover how you can make sure you shine like a true professional during an interview.

Chapter 7

How to shine in interviews

Eight ways to make a good impression on journalists

As we have seen, you will be meeting journalists under a number of different circumstances. There will be special points to bear in mind for some of those circumstances. But there are also a number of general rules for creating a good impression with journalists.

Some of these rules seem like common-sense. But they are mentioned because they have all been broken at some time – in certain instances, many times – by spokespeople meeting journalists. There are eight key points to bear in mind if you want to develop good "interview manners".

1 If you have arranged a meeting with a journalist, keep it. Turn up. Don't send along a deputy. The journalist has come to see the organ grinder – not the monkey.

2 If you have arranged a meeting with a journalist don't keep him or her waiting. You may think you give an impression of a very important person grappling with big issues while the journalist waits in reception. But you don't. You just create an image of bad-mannered boorishness. And you almost certainly get the interview off to a poor start. If punctuality is the politeness of princes, it should be of interviewees as well.

3 A friendly greeting works wonders. It creates immediate empathy. It marks you out as one of nature's warm-hearted people. It shows you're looking forward to the meeting and expect it to be useful. So cross the room to greet your interviewer. Get up from

behind your desk with a smile on your face and your hand out-stretched for a firm shake.

4 Adopt a positive, helpful attitude. The journalist wants to meet you and find out about your organisation. Act as though you want to meet him or her. Not as if the interview is an unwelcome intrusion in a busy day. (Even if it is.)

5 Give all your time to your interviewer. Put calls on hold. Tell your secretary to keep personal visitors in the outer office. Don't sit scanning e-mails or text messages while answering questions. Don't seem bored. Or rushed. Or look as though there are more important things you could be doing.

6 Make sure you meet in a setting that will do you credit.If your office is small and untidy, reserve a meeting room.Remember, the journalists can write about what they see as well as about what you tell them. If you don't want it mentioned, take those pictures of your five previous spouses off your desk!

7 Behave in a way that portrays the style you want to convey – for example, in the way you treat other members of staff the journalist meets while he or she is with you. And in your approach to drivers, doormen and waiters. (Journalists are like receptionists in that they can usually tell who the "nice people" are.)

8 Moderation pays dividends. Don't use language that would make a sailor blush – especially with female journalists (although there are one or two who could, themselves, redden the cheeks of most of the Royal Navy). If entertainment is involved, drink moderately. Even if the journalist doesn't.

The essential elements of good interviewee technique
Being a good interviewee is not a God-given gift. It is something that can be learned and developed. Nor is there anything mysteri-

ous about it. In a world in which every kind of organisation – corporation, public authority, charity, non-governmental organisation – has to put its point of view, ability as an interviewee is another important communication skill.

It is important to stress that there are very few "natural" interviewees. And there is, after all, no reason why being a skilled interviewee should come any more naturally than being a skilled accountant or any other specialist task. With knowledge, technique and training you can become an effective interviewee. In being a good interviewee, you need to give attention to three main areas. We will deal with each of them in turn.

1 *What to do during an interview to be more effective.*

During an interview, you should seek to follow the guidelines in checklist 35.

Checklist 35: 12 fundamental rules for interviews

- Tell the truth. Never be caught in a lie – and, if you try one, you surely will be. The journalist will never completely believe you again.
- Keep to the point. If you have done the preparation suggested in the earlier chapters you will know what your point is. Keep to it. Don't wander off or be distracted. If you establish a clear focus, an interviewer will often respond with further questions in that area.
- Be sure of your facts. Only provide information that you're certain about. Having to back-track to correct yourself only undermines your authority as an interviewee.
- Be positive and direct. Use positive angles for your story. Even if there is a negative aspect to the story, accentuate the

positive elements. But avoid unrealistic hype. Or claims you cannot substantiate.

- Keep your message simple. Simple messages make the most impact. Few people have the time or inclination to digest the minutiae of a finely developed case.
- Be informed and spontaneous. You will be well briefed, but don't sound as though you are parroting an official line. Sound as though you actually believe what you're saying. And clearly understand the parameters of the information you want to give – and the information you don't.
- Light up your message. Use examples, anecdotes or stories to bring your message to life. Try to have some well-turned phrases to bring your message home powerfully. (But don't use over-the-top language you can't substantiate.)
- Let your voice sell your message. Don't speak in a monotone. Adopt the right tone of voice for the message you're giving – in the way you do in ordinary life. But don't try to be theatrical. That will sound false.
- Be brief and clear. When you've made your point stop. Don't ramble. And don't be ambiguous in your answers. Eschew jargon. Make it clear what you mean.
- Use the questions as pegs for your answers. Use the questions to steer towards what you want to say. That means you must listen carefully to the questions and catch any nuances behind them. But don't tell the interviewer what questions to ask. And don't start cross-questioning the interviewer.
- Look at your interviewer. Talk to him or her. Eye contact increases rapport between you. And it makes you appear open and honest. (Which, of course, you are.)
- Tackle distortions or untruths at once. Don't allow the

interviewer to summarise your answers in a way that is not completely accurate or gives your answer an emphasis you didn't intend. Make clear what you mean and what the truth is. ▪

One issue that needs to be dealt with at more length is whether or not to speak "off the record". Unless you know the journalist well and trust him or her, beware of doing this. Even then, be cautious. Off the record means that what you say is to guide the reporter but should not be written. But off-the-record information is known to find its way into stories. Above all, never tell a journalist something – and then add as an after-thought that it was "off the record". As a general rule of thumb follow these three guidelines:

- If you don't know the journalist or only know him or her slightly, it is probably wisest only to give "off the record" information when the alternative is worse. For instance, when "off the record" information can defuse a potentially damaging story by providing the journalist with an understanding of background facts that change his or her perception of it.
- If you know the journalist well and have developed mutual trust, you can use "off the record" comments to steer him or her towards a story that may aid your organisation's objectives, but with which you would not want to be directly connected.
- But it is worth remembering that some journalists prefer not to have off the record information. They might find the information elsewhere, and they want to be completely free to use it.

Finally, remember that providing "off the record" information in any situation entails risks. You have to make a judgement as to whether those risks are worth taking given the situation you are in.

2 *What not to do during an interview*. Interviews can, and do, go wrong. But there are a number of common mistakes that people make when interviewed by journalists. The mistakes are summarised in checklist 36.

Checklist 36: five mistakes to avoid in an interview

- Don't give a journalist information "not for attribution", except when you are confident the journalist will use it in a way that cannot be traced back to you. The information might not be attributed to you by name. But it could be attributed to the "company", a "government spokesman" a "well placed source" or some similar phrase which identifies you indirectly to those in the know.

- Don't "shoot from the hip". You don't have to say the first thing that comes into your mind. If you're asked a tricky question, consider your answer before giving it. If it's a particularly sensitive area, make it clear to the journalist that you want to think about the point before answering.

- Don't get drawn into areas you don't want to talk about. If the journalist raises subjects you're not happy about discussing – for instance, about the business prospects of competitors or your views on elected or public officials – don't be drawn. The journalist may be persistent. (He or she may try to second-guess you – What will your profit be next year? Will it be more than £10m? More than £20m?) But you must be politely firm.

- Don't be arrogant or pompous. You may be an important captain of industry or head of a department in a large organisation, used to commanding legions of minions. But don't show it. In an interview, a touch of humility serves you well. Don't interrupt when you're being asked questions. And on no account, tell the journalist what questions to ask you.

- Never say: "No comment". In most cases, its tantamount to admitting guilt. Choose a form of words that explains why you can't comment. For example: "We haven't decided that yet." Or: "We won't be announcing that until next week." ▪

3 *How to handle journalists' ploys that might trap you.* News has been defined as something that somebody doesn't want to tell you. And sometimes it may seem to you that a journalist is more interested in what you don't want to tell him or her than what you do. They can use a number of ploys to tempt you to tell them more than you meant. These ploys are summarised in checklist 37.

Checklist 37: nine ploys journalists use to trap you

- The big yawn. Beware of the journalist who doesn't seem interested in what you're saying. He knows it'll tempt you to make what you're saying more interesting. And to do it you might reveal facts you meant to keep confidential.
- The closed notebook. Just because the journalist shuts his notebook doesn't mean the interview is over. He's still listening to what you are saying. And he can use it in his article.
- The "manufactured" quote. That's when the journalist tries to put words into your mouth. The journalist starts a question with words like: "Wouldn't you agree that..." and follows it up with some tendentious comments. Never answer a leading question of the "manufactured quote" variety with a simple "yes" or "no" . "Yes" could be taken as agreement with the

proposition. "No" could be interpreted in a way that you don't regard the subject as important. You should say something like: "I wouldn't use those words…" And then add: "The way I would put it…" saying what you mean in words you feel comfortable with. How to spot these loaded questions? They often contain words like "blame", "condemn", "accuse", etc.

- The upside down reader. If you're consulting documents during your interview – or have other documents on your desk – make sure they are not confidential. Many journalists, particularly the older ones who were trained in the ancient art of "subbing on the stone" are experts at reading upside down.

- The shoulder to cry on. A journalist may seem sympathetic to your organisation and your personal concerns. However, do not treat a journalist – especially over informal drinks afterwards – as a confidante or sympathetic ear for worries or concerns you have about your job, your colleagues or your organisation.

- The red rag. Don't charge at it when it's waved at you. That's what the journalist wants you to do. If a journalist asks what seem rude or hostile questions, he may try to provoke you into losing your temper. You might say something then you'd later regret to see in print.

- The smooth talker. Virtually the opposite of the "red rag". The journalist suggests that you're a "man of the world" or a "discerning woman" or that you're too clever to believe "all that". And then asks: "So what's the real story?" Stick to your guns.

- The bush beater. A journalist may seem to be spending a lot of time repeating questions in slightly different ways – beating about the bush – or asking similar questions. He or she keeps coming at the same subject from different directions. By worrying away at a topic like this, the journalist is hoping to lull you into a false sense of security. He or she may be trying to extract contradictory answers that could be used as the basis for further probing questions. Stick to your guns. Repeat yourself if necessary – and try to move the discussion on by revealing in your answers other interesting areas you would like to discuss.

• The "when did you stop beating your wife?" question. There could be some occasions when a journalist will make an accusation – perhaps repeated from another source – which you know to be totally false. But by denying it you could give credence to the allegation. More importantly, you could give the journalist a reason for writing a story of the "Managers/ officials today denied…" variety. What to do? Insist on going "off the record" straight away. Provide the facts to show there is no story. Even if the journalist threatens to run a story saying you declined to comment, keep your counsel. Anything you say on the record will help to prop up the story. And, in many instances, the lack of a suitable quote from you may kill the story anyway, especially if you explained off the record that the premise is wrong anyway. ■

What to do in 10 different kinds of interviews

In chapter six, we identified a number of different situations in which you could meet the media. We now need to look at the special circumstances that apply in each of them. We have already dealt with what you need to know in order to deal with face-to-face interviews in this chapter. Guidelines for each of the other main areas are contained in checklists 38 to 48.

Telephone interviews. Journalists do much of their information gathering on the telephone. It is an instrument they are very skilled at using. If you are acting as a spokesperson, it is highly probable that you will speak to journalists more frequently on the telephone than in any other situation. So bear in mind the points in checklist 38.

Checklist 38: eight ways to score in telephone interviews

- Decide who should handle the query. When a journalist phones with a query, ask yourself whether you are the right person to comment. Or should someone else deal with the query? But don't use that as an excuse for not talking to a journalist, when it is your responsibility. And don't refuse to talk to a journalist just because he or she is on the telephone.
- Be available. For journalists up against deadlines, there is nothing more frustrating than people who are always "in meetings" . If it's at all possible come out of the meeting to take the call. If you can't, find out when the journalist's deadline expires and call back at the earliest opportunity. Make sure that secretaries and switchboard operators are briefed on how to deal with calls from the media and when to interrupt meetings.
- Have key information ready. Before you launch into the detail of the interview, find out this important information: journalist's name, publication/broadcasting organisation, why he/she is calling you, contact number, whether the interview is on the record or attributable (remember earlier advice).
- Be aware of the dangers of telephone interviews. Because you cannot see your interviewer this could make you more

talkative than is usual. Combat the danger of garrulousness by imagining you are talking in front of a colleague.

• Keep in mind the lack of face to face contact. On the telephone there is no "body language" to give special emphasis to parts of your message. Nor can you use facial expressions to give shades of meaning to what you say. So make sure everything is crystal clear. Humour, too, can more easily be misinterpreted on the phone because there is no body language to signal it.

• Don't be rushed. Take your time to think. If necessary, note the question and offer to call back. Consider your response. Get a colleague's view. Make sure you do call back.

• Don't say things for the sake of it. A busy journalist with a deadline to meet will resent having his or her time wasted. If you've nothing useful to say on the proposed interview topic, say so. Explain why.

• Call back. If you think of something else after the interview has finished, ring again. The reporter will be pleased to hear from you providing you do have useful extra information to give and it is before the deadline expires. ■

(One category of telephone interview that is becoming more common is the telephone interview with a radio station. For further information about this, see chapter eight.)

Checklist 39: six ways to score in a conference call interview

• Treat the call as a team effort in which everybody involved has a contribution to make. Don't let one person do all the talking – the journalist will wonder what the point of the other people is.

- Plan in advance who is going to cover which topics. Failing to do so can lead to confusion during the interview. Even worse, it can lead to rivalry as individuals seek to butt in with their own views.

- Ensure the technical aspects work. There are several different ways of organising conference calls, most of which work very well most of the time. But make sure that any areas of technical weakness are covered. The most common problems arise with a speaker microphone used by several people in the same room. Too far away, and the journalist won't hear clearly what you're saying. Even close up, speaker microphones can distort voices which may make it difficult for the journalist to hear names and/or technical terms correctly.

- Don't all speak at once. Work out who is going to speak first and how the interview will proceed with the other people in the conference.

- Don't air differences in the conference. You should have sorted out any contentious points before the conference starts. Don't argue about points of difference while the conference is taking place. You may be giving the journalist a story he or she didn't expect.

- Follow up the conference by providing additional information on points not fully covered in the conference. You can do this by ordinary telephone call or e-mail. ■

Checklist 40: seven ways to score in an e-mail interview

- Understand the purpose of the interview. This is important in all interviews, but is especially important with e-mail where there is no personal or telephone contact.

- Be clear about what the information you provide will be used for. Is it merely for background or is the journalist looking for quotes to use in his/her story?
- Ask for clarification before you answer confusing questions. If you don't understand a question, seek e-mail clarification before answering it. At best, this avoids you annoying the journalist with unwanted information. At worst, it means you avoid giving information which perhaps you would have rather kept quiet about.
- Answer questions fully but briefly. E-mail tempts people to write at speed and ramble. You need to make sure that you provide the information that's asked for but do so in a succinct way.
- Be precise and accurate. Because e-mail is an informal medium, people often tend to be casual with the way in which they provide information. This may be acceptable for an ordinary exchange. You need to treat information in an e-mail interview as carefully as information you would provide in any other form of interview. Pay attention to factual accuracy.
- Don't use slang or "e-mail English". This won't look good if it's quoted. Answer questions in simple straightforward English, paying due attention to spelling, grammar and punctuation.
- Answer follow-up queries politely where you have extra relevant information. If you don't have any more information to give, e-mail back to say so. Don't be drawn in to giving information you wish to keep confidential. ■

Press conferences. A press conference could be called by your organisation in order to make an announcement. Or it could be called in response to a large number of requests from journalists for information about a particular topic or incident – for example, in a crisis. The guidelines in checklist 41 are more applicable to the kind of situation where your organisation is making a proactive announcement rather than reacting to a crisis. (For information on dealing with a crisis, see chapter nine.)

These guidelines do not set out to describe how to organise a press conference. The public relations professional should be able to advise on that and handle arrangements. Instead, the guidelines are intended to make you, as a spokesperson at the conference, more effective.

Checklist 41: 10 ways to score at a press conference

- Be clear about the purpose of the conference. Know what messages you want to get across. (If necessary, refer back to chapter five on creating memorable messages.) Make sure that all participating managers understand what part they must play in formulating and delivering the messages that will be conveyed at the press conference. Be clear what you have to do. Know what others are doing and how you fit into the overall plan of the conference.
- Thoroughly prepare your presentation. Check with other speakers that you're not covering the same ground. Remember you're talking to journalists, not potential customers. They are looking for news. (For more advice on preparing a press conference presentation, see checklist 42.)
- Make sure you have a clearly readable script or notes. If you have a script, don't read it. Learn it thoroughly, so you only have to refer to it. If you use notes, set them out clearly and make sure all points, facts and examples are included.

- Prepare any visual aids. Make sure they add something to, rather than just repeat, what you're saying. Keep them simple.
- Anticipate any questions you may be asked. Prepare model answers. Be aware of any difficult or sensitive areas and plan with other managers who will be at the conference how to handle them.
- Rehearse your speech. Preferably in the room in which you'll be giving it. Check its timing. Don't overrun.
- Check your visual aids. Then check them again. And a third time just before you begin. Make sure the equipment you'll be using works and you know how to use it – including the microphone if there is one.
- When making your presentation, speak up. Don't mumble.
- Don't be put off. It may look as though your audience of journalists is paying little interest. Don't worry: they're taking it all in. They're not there to cheer. They like to play their cards close to their chest.
- At question time keep calm. Don't be flummoxed by seemingly hostile questions. They're just probing. If you've prepared well, you'll know your answers. ■

Checklist 42: seven key points for preparing a press conference presentation

- Put the main point at the front.
- Keep it hard and newsworthy, avoiding irrelevant background information or self-congratulation.
- Eschew jargon, sales talk and organisation-speak.
- Pack your talk with interesting facts and examples.

- Keep the pace right – don't have so little material that people will feel bored or cheated, or put in so many points that you will need to talk so fast that people do not have time to register, absorb and record what you are saying.
- Keep to your time limit: not more than 10 to 15 minutes.
- Beware of humour: it can fall flat.

Press briefings. Because a press briefing, with its small numbers, is less formal than a press conference – it often takes place over lunch, dinner, breakfast (or even just a cup of coffee or a drink). Whichever, it requires a special style.

Checklist 43: five ways to score at a press briefing

- Know who's coming. Make sure you have the key information about the journalists who will be present.
- Tailor your messages specifically for each of the journalists who will be present. Try to look at your message from the different angles they'll approach it. And be ready to talk about it in those terms.
- Apportion your time. At the event, spend a fair amount of time with each journalist. Don't monopolise one or allow yourself to be monopolised by one. After a fair time, politely extricate yourself and move on to the next person.
- Be aware of the danger of going beyond your brief. Especially in the relaxed post-prandial atmosphere of a lunch or dinner.
- Don't provide accidental quotes through throw-away lines you thought weren't being noted down. And, remember, you're not there to be amusing or entertaining but to achieve a purpose. (That doesn't mean you can't be amusing and entertaining in

the service of your purpose.) ▦

Facility trip or visit. This is not a workbook on how to organise a facility trip or press visit. Again, that is a task for the public relations professional. If, as a spokesperson for your organisation, you are involved in one, remember the points in checklist 44.

Checklist 44: five ways to score during a facility trip or visit

- Know who's coming. Brief yourself using background information you've compiled on invited journalists and their publications/broadcasting outlets. Prepare to tailor any messages or information you have to give to them.
- Thoroughly brief any third parties. That includes managers in sites visited, customers, user sites, etc. They need to know what's happening, who's coming and to be helped to develop their own messages so that they dovetail with your own.
- Rehearse demonstrations. Don't assume something will work just because it always has. And have a fall-back position if something goes wrong. In the case of any outdoor activities make contingency arrangements for possible bad weather.
- Be friendly to your journalist guests. But be aware of the dangers of allowing yourself to give away more information than you meant to.
- Provide the same standard of travel and accommodation facilities for the journalists as for yourself. ▦

Exhibition. If you have a stand at an exhibition, your public relations advisers will probably arrange to provide journalists with information in the press office. As a spokesperson, who may be interviewed by journalists at the exhibition, you need to follow the advice in checklist 45.

Checklist 45: seven ways to score at an exhibition

- Make sure everyone on your stand knows what to do if approached by a journalist. It is sometimes best if certain individuals are designated with the task of talking to journalists.
- Make sure those tasked with talking to journalists are briefed thoroughly on the messages that are to be put across. If several people are talking to journalists, it is important that they "sing from the same song sheet". Make sure they all know what's news – new products, new customers, new membership services, etc.
- Have spare press kits on the stand. Journalists might not have picked it out from among (possibly) hundreds in the press room.
- Make sure those briefed to talk to journalists can be reached easily on their mobiles. If necessary, organise a rota so that the stand is always manned by a press spokesperson.
- When a journalist calls on the stand get his/her name, publication and contact number. Don't lose the information in the stand clutter.
- Take time with journalists on the stand. Don't make them feel rushed. Or treat them as second-class citizens compared with potential customers.
- Make sure everyone on the stand is aware of the danger of careless talk. That means everyone from the most junior to the most senior. Overheard comments can give reporters interesting leads into stories you might prefer they didn't know about. ▪

Checklist 46: five ways to score at annual general meetings

- If you want to use the occasion to address the broader world, make sure you give your remarks a sharp news edge. Have something positive to say. Quote facts and figures.
- Brief yourself on potential areas of difficulty. Be aware of disgruntled shareholders or members out to cause trouble. Handle them with care. Don't let the press treat any confrontation as a David and Goliath incident, with you as the unfriendly Goliath.
- Prepare an abstract of the main points of your message and statement. At certain times of year, financial journalists and editors are inundated with annual reports and accounts – they may not have time to search yours for the main points.
- Do not hold the AGM too late in the day. The journalists may not have time to file their stories for the following day's papers. (And, by the day after, you're old news.)
- At a major event, consider providing one or more interview rooms. These can be used for one-to-one interviews with journalists. ▨

Conference or seminar. Addressing an industry or professional conference or seminar can be interesting and potentially useful. But keep in mind the points in checklist 47.

Checklist 47: four ways to score at a conference or seminar

- Find out whether journalists are going to be present. If so, you may need to tailor your remarks accordingly.
- Be helpful to the press if you want to generate press coverage. Provide a copy of your speech. Be available for a follow-up

interview to provide further information or background after it.

- Be careful about ambiguity or vagueness. When journalists are looking for a popular angle in a technical or semi-technical presentation, they can easily get the wrong end of the stick. So be quite clear about what you're saying.
- Answer questions with care. If journalists are in the audience you may be limited in the information you can provide in answers – especially about confidential plans, certain internal matters, customers or members. ▨

Door-stepping. Door-stepping – the practise of reporters hanging around your house or office in order to question you as you come and go – normally only happens when things are going wrong. You can handle this difficult situation by following the guidelines in checklist 48.

Checklist 48: seven ways to score if you're door-stepped

- Come and go with dignity. Don't try to sneak out of back-ways. The media will have them covered. Don't run away down the street. Don't shield your face with newspapers. Your calm dignity will show you're still in command of the situation.
- Before you leave or arrive, decide if you want to say anything. If not, just say "good morning" , "nice day" , etc. Don't get provoked into making short angry comments.
- If you do decide to speak, work out precisely what you want to say. Then stick to it. Don't get drawn further, no matter how persistent the questioning.
- When you speak, stop and talk. Don't be questioned on the

move – especially if film or video cameras are present. But when you've said your piece, move purposefully onward.

- Be neatly presented and smartly dressed. Shabby personal appearance creates a bad impression at any time – but especially when you're trying to win sympathy. You could also give an impression of being under pressure and not coping.
- Be confident. Appear in control of the situation.
- Don't get hostile. Of course, journalists may intrude on your privacy. But you may just have to put up with this. By being friendly or even stoical you can win public sympathy. ▨

Making a picture worth a thousand words

Very few people, outside the high-pressure world of professional models, seem to enjoy having their photograph taken. Yet newspapers and magazines use thousands of pictures every day – so they provide an important publicity opportunity. But what too many spokespeople fail to realise is that the picture accompanying an article is an important part of the message. In some cases, it could be the most important part of the message. The old proverb about a picture being worth a thousand words is still true in the media. Indeed, in many newspapers and magazines, a picture occupies more space than a thousand words! The picture will certainly be the first part of the message noticed by the reader of the newspaper or magazine.

Some photographers are extremely skilled in taking pictures which portray what they perceive to be the character of the person they're photographing. Indeed, the best photographers have many tricks for getting people to reveal their character during photoshoots. It is important, therefore, that you should devote enough time to any necessary photography – and not treat it as an irritating afterthought – if you want to be shown at your best.

It is especially important to consider ways in which you can help to make any photograph underline your message – for example, by being photographed using your product, visiting the new building, meeting customers or members. To get the best results, follow the guidelines in checklist 49.

Checklist 49: nine ways to be photographed at your best

- Be co-operative. Help the photographer to get the best picture of you. Don't object if he draws your curtains, moves your chair, or shifts around objects on your desk. He's trying to get the best lighting condition and remove distracting clutter.
- But don't be manipulated. The photographer may want to take an unusual shot. Perhaps with a backdrop of your product or factory. Be sure that it is something you'll be happy with.
- Don't be shy. Check your clothes and hair. Look the part.
- Avoid an audience. You don't need wise-cracking colleagues looking on.
- Offer more than a stock shot if you're asked to send a photograph. Newspapers and magazines keep stock head and shoulder shots (the boardroom portrait) on file and sometimes specifically request them. But they are increasingly looking for something more creative. If you can provide it, you can get your picture used ahead of others.
- Keep your face animated when being photographed. But without pulling odd expressions. Politicians, for example, like to be photographed talking because, apart from the fact it's what they do well, it makes their face look alive.
- If standing up don't be rigid. Or adopt an awkward posture.

Hold that middle-aged spread in.

- In groups, stand close together. It makes the tight shot editors like. And although it may feel strange, it won't look it in the picture.
- Relax. ▒

So far, we've looked at how you can perform at your peak in interviews with print journalists. Much of the advice is true for any kind of interview you undertake. But, when it comes to appearing on radio or television, there are also other important factors you have to consider.

CHAPTER 8

HOW TO MAKE YOUR MARK ON RADIO AND TELEVISION

How to develop a broadcasting policy for your organisation

In most cases, you are still likely to be interviewed by print journalists. But it is becoming more likely that you may be interviewed on television or, more probably, radio. The possibility of a radio or television interview is something that you should not ignore. There are three reasons for it.

1 It is a simple question of quantity. There is now more broadcasting than ever before. More radio stations – especially local stations. And more television stations. Further, they are broadcasting for longer. They need programmes about all sorts of topics to fill up the airwaves.

2 The growth of broadcast media has spawned a new approach to programming – "narrowcasting". When there was only a handful of terrestrial television stations, they needed to devote most of their broadcasting time to capturing mass audiences. Now that there are so many hours of broadcasting available from so many satellite and cable channels, they can devote more time to appealing to specialised niche audiences. Hence, narrowcasting. No wonder that more people from many different walks of life now find they may have an opportunity to appear on radio or television.

3 Even if you are not invited to appear on television or radio, you could still find yourself drafted in to appear in a webcast or videoconference. In both cases, broadcasting skills will help you put across your case to a remote audience.

But before you comb your hair, apply some make-up and step before a camera, it is vital that your organisation develops a broadcast media policy that determines at least:

- When you will allow representatives from your organisation to appear on radio and television.
- When and where you will allow cameras on your organisation's premises.
- Who is allowed to represent the organisation on radio and television – and under what circumstances.

In order to develop such a policy it is first necessary to be aware of the different circumstances in which you and your organisation could conceivably be invited on to television or radio. Checklists 50 and 51 set these out in general terms.

Checklist 50: eight ways you could appear on television

News programmes (national or regional)
- Studio interview (live or recorded).
- Location interview (at your home/offices or elsewhere).
- Down-the-line interview (you are interviewed from a remote location by an interviewer in the studio).
- Telephone interview (rare on television, but occasionally done). You speak to an interviewer over the telephone while a picture of you or your organisation's office or something else relevant is on screen.
- Quoted comments (you speak to a reporter who quotes your comments in a scripted news broadcast).

Documentary/actuality programmes
- Studio interview (generally recorded or live).

- Location interview (generally recorded on your premises or elsewhere).
- Studio discussion (recorded or live, generally with a panel, and sometimes with an audience). ■

Checklist 51: nine ways you could appear on radio

News programmes
- Studio interview (recorded or live).
- Location interview (invariably recorded at your premises or another location).
- Telephone interview (at an arranged time you speak to a studio interviewer over a telephone line).
- Quoted comments (you speak to a reporter who quotes your comments in a scripted news item).

Documentary/actuality programming
- Studio interview (either recorded or live).
- Location interview (normally recorded).
- Studio discussion (often with other members and either recorded or live).
- Quoted comments (you speak to a reporter or researcher who quotes your comments in the programme).

Phone-ins
- Studio-based (you answer questions live from an interviewer and members of the public over the telephone). ■

With the information in checklists 50 and 51 in mind, you are now in a position to develop a broadcasting policy for your organisation. The elements contained in such a policy will vary quite considerably from one organisation to another. The detail of your organisation's policy will be determined by factors such as the three mentioned below:

- the size of your organisation.
- the likelihood of your leading figures being invited to take part in broadcast opportunities, which will depend on factors such as your organisation's profile, the extent to which it is already on the broadcasters' radar screen, and whether it is operating in an area of controversy or public interest.
- and your organisation's sensitivity to matters broadcast about its activities.

Three points need to be made quite clear:

1 It may be possible to find or generate proactive opportunities for positive coverage of your organisation and its activities. But how much coverage you are likely to be able to generate and on what programmes will obviously vary very considerably from one organisation to another. However, the proliferation of broadcast media means that there are now more opportunities than ever, and organisations which would have stood very little chance of receiving radio or television coverage 20 or even 10 years ago can now grab their moments of on-air glory.

2 It is important to bear in mind, though, that invitations to take part in a radio or television programme invariably come on the broadcasters' own terms. Often, the programme's editor, director or producer may have already developed an editorial line for the programme they plan to make. This line may or may not be helpful to the kinds of messages you would want to put across on air.

3 There may also be times when the broadcast media is interested in a story that is not helpful to your organisation's image

or objectives. In these cases, there is no point imagining that if you ignore the broadcast media they will go away and not bother you. You need to meet the challenge and seek to limit the damage.

With these three points, use the questions in checklist 52 as a guide when drawing up your own organisation's broadcasting policy.

Checklist 52: three key issues when deciding on a broadcasting policy

A Spokespeople:
Who is allowed to speak on-air on:
- any issue?
- financial issues?
- governance, regulatory and/or legal issues?
- people issues?
- product/service issues?
- community issues?
- labour relations?
- environmental/green issues?
- other categories specific to your organisation?
- crisis spokesperson is:

B Training
- Have spokespeople been trained to appear in the media?
- Is media training provided when people change jobs and new people join?
- What additional training do specific spokespeople need?
- Are both training and spokesperson skills that have been acquired kept up to date?

C Facility filming

- Are cameras allowed onto your premises?
- In which buildings or areas are cameras not allowed?
- What conditions will be applied to filming on the premises?
- Who is authorised to give permission for filming?
- Who ensures health and safety and any public liability issues are covered?
- Will we supply products for filming elsewhere? ■

Finally, when you have drawn up your broadcasting policy make sure that everybody in your organisation who needs to know about it does know about it. The policy should be written down and circulated to those people who may take decisions, so that there is no doubt or confusion over what the policy is.

How to set the ground rules for broadcast interviews

As with most types of interviews, there are three kinds of situations on television and radio:

- Pro-active: where you are putting across a positive message.
- Re-active: where you are responding to requests for information or comment. In broadcasting, this can mean defending yourself or your organisation against criticism – but you may be asked to comment on an issue as a result of the specialised knowledge that you have.
- Crisis: where you are providing information in response to a dramatic event – sometimes a disaster. (This is dealt with specifically in chapter nine, Communicating in Crisis.)

It is, of course, important to prepare for all types of interview. Indeed, it is especially important that you prepare for what you imagine will be the positive kind of interview. Far too many spokespeople have shot themselves in the foot because they thought that what seemed like a positive opportunity was going to be an easy ride.

However, it is also the case that there is an increasing number of occasions on both television and radio when a spokesperson has to defend his or her organisation against criticism or allegations. Both television and radio lend themselves to a more dramatic adversarial approach to news and features than print journalism. And there is a growing interest both from news programmes and documentaries for "investigative" stories.

The first thing to remember if your organisation is targeted by an investigative programme with a potentially negative impact is that you are not powerless. So instead of sitting transfixed like a snake mesmerised by a mongoose, you should act to ensure that your company is presented in the best possible light. You need to set the ground rules for any interviews or facility filming that might be required at your organisation.

The first step is to find out what the programme is about and what specific interest the programme makers have in your organisation. You should also ask them why they want an interview or filming facilities. And it does no harm at all to ask them to put that information in writing if you have any genuine cause to doubt their motives. You both then know where you stand.

The second step is to decide whether you want to take part in the proposed programme. As a general rule, if specific criticisms are to be levelled against your organisation, there are very few cases when you should decline an invitation to take part outright. In those cases, the programme makers will almost always state in their programme that you refused to take part and the refusal may be presented in such a way as to make you or your organisation appear in a negative light.

In fact, it is arguably your duty to your organisation – however difficult or troublesome – to co-operate with the programme makers and make sure that your organisation's case is put in as positive a manner as possible. In doing this, it is helpful to adopt the following four-point approach:

1 Be certain you are fully aware of as many facts about the programme/news item as possible.

2 Prepare a thorough background briefing about the topic from your organisation's point of view.

3 Share your background research with the programme makers in order to influence or alter their perspective of the issue. (See checklist 55 for more on this point.)

4 Establish clearly what control, if any, you will have over your contribution to the programme.

Checklists 53 to 56 set out specific questions you should ask yourself as you deal with each of these four points.

Checklist 53: nine facts you must know about a programme on your organisation

- What precisely will the programme be dealing with?
- Why was this subject chosen? What events or circumstances have brought it about?
- What is the editorial point of view of the programme and/or presenter?
- In what context will the items in question appear?
- Who else (especially critics) will be given air time in the programme?
- What specific allegations/criticisms are likely to be made

about your organisation?

- When will the programme be broadcast?
- Who is likely to see/hear it?
- What groups or interested parties could have strong feelings, on the matter – who could you possibly annoy?

Checklist 54: eight facts you must know about a programme dealing with specific allegations about your organisation

- What are the precise facts of the case?
- What policies and/or objectives are at stake?
- How has the situation arisen?
- What is the background history to the situation?
- What research, etc exists that throws light on the situation?
- What is the organisation on record as having said about the issue?
- What is the experience of other organisations in this country and abroad in a similar situation to our own?
- Are there any special circumstances, such as a legal case pending or an investigation in process, that would not make it appropriate to comment?

Checklist 55: six reasons for sharing research with programme makers

- Remember that programme makers have a duty to be fair and only to make criticisms/allegations in the light of known facts. (If they don't know the true facts they might make the allegations out of ignorance rather than malice.)
- Even someone with an entrenched point of view can't argue with facts when those facts show their view to be erroneous.

- Programme makers usually want to get the true facts. They don't want to present a point of view that is later shown to be at fault.
- Co-operating fully, even – perhaps especially – when you are under attack, wins goodwill and sympathy when it's your turn to have your say.
- But don't confuse journalists/researchers with too much detail. Concentrate on the points you want to correct and marshal all information to that aim.
- If you have agreed to be interviewed, keep something up your sleeve for the interview. Don't let it out in advance – especially any bull points you will make to rebut known criticisms. ■

Checklist 56: three ground rules for programme participation

- In a feature programme, will you have the opportunity to view the programme before it is broadcast in order to see how your contribution is presented in relation to others?
- In the case of extremely sensitive issues, it may be essential to make this a pre-condition of taking part in the programme.
- In exceptional circumstances, it may be necessary to get your lawyers to draw up an agreement with the broadcasting authorities to entrench your rights to view the programme before transmission and to insist on a change to any section of your interview that you feel has been unfairly presented due to editing or unreasonable juxtaposition with other matter. ■

As you will see, doing all the work set out in checklists 53 to 56 could take up considerable time and effort – not to mention money. However, not to do it could be to invite disaster. The nature of broadcasting is such that a casual approach almost always ends in you finding yourself or your organisation presented in a way which is unhelpful at best or damaging at worst.

How to prepare well for a radio or television interview

In preparing to put your message across effectively in a radio or television interview, there are two main areas you need to consider.

1 The actual circumstances of the interview – and how you can turn them to your advantage.

Before you step before the cameras, it is important that you should know what is going to happen and how. You need to know:

Whether the interview will take place in a studio or on location. In general an interview that takes place in a studio or calm office is better than an interview that takes place in the street, on the doorstep or some other public spot. For a start, you will have far fewer distractions – and, in many cases, so will the viewer (no people pulling funny faces behind the camera!). You should not agree to do the interview in any place that you feel uncomfortable about. And you should be especially wary of allowing the interviewer to manoeuvre you into a position which will show you in an embarrassing or poor light. In cases where what is happening outside is the main point of the story – and usually when the story is a positive one – then there is a stronger case for conducting the interview out of doors at a relevant location. Indeed, there could be occasions where the location is an important part of the story. In those cases, being interviewed in the location which helps to make your point makes sense both from the broadcaster's and your point of view.

Whether you will be interviewed alone or with others. If you are being interviewed with someone else, the chances are that the other person is there to provide an alternative view. You need to know who they are and the points they might make so that you are ready to counter them.

How long the proposed interview will be. This will influence the way you present your message. If you know that television will show only a 10 second clip of you, there is no point in preparing a detailed case. You need a carefully crafted one sentence "sound bite" that gets your central point across. On the other hand, if you're taking part in the kind of lengthier interview which longer news programmes now frequently run, perhaps lasting from three to six minutes, you need to have information in depth to deploy during the interview, even though you should still make individual points simply and briefly.

Who the interviewer will be. Different interviewers have different styles – and pet hobby-horses – so it is useful to be aware of these in advance.

Whether the interview will be live or taped. On both radio and television, a live interview creates immediate impact, but leaves you with little or no control. There is, obviously, no chance of editing after the event. (But that cuts both ways for the interviewer and the interviewee.) In a live interview, it is essential that you get your message across in the time available. When the time is up, the interviewer will cut you off, whether you've finished or not. A recorded interview can be edited, which means that some of your comments can be cut. But with a recorded interview there is always the possibility of doing it again, given the goodwill of the interviewer, which may not always be forthcoming. Similarly, a taped interview can also be edited. If you are being recorded and the programme maker is going to add a commentary after, it is useful to know what that commentary will be about. It could, for example, be something critical.

2 *The points you want to put across in your interview – and the way to put them across most effectively.*

Even in a two- to three-minute interview, you will not have time to make more than a couple of points – three at the most. In a 40-second interview, you can realistically make only one point. And, it must be added, in an even shorter "sound bite" you might only have time for one sentence. All this means that you simply cannot afford to step before the cameras unprepared. You must know what you want to say in advance – and how you are going to say it. Checklist 57 suggests a way of preparing what you want to say in a broadcast interview.

> ### Checklist 57: six ways to prepare what you'll say on radio or television

- First, write down in not more than 20 words each of the three most important points you want to make.
- Look at them. Are you sure they are the three most important points. (While you do this, consider the audience you'll be reaching. Look at what you have to say from their point of view.)
- Next, decide which key facts or examples support your main points. Again, be brief. One fact or simple example for each point.
- Work out how you can use that fact or example to get across your point. Use simple direct language. Are your points clear, forceful and unambiguous? Are they in tune with your organisation's policy?

- Make a note of likely questions you could be asked. Work out how in answering those questions you could make the key points you have already defined. What is the question you would least like to be asked? How would you answer it?
- Finally, what is your most important point? If you only get the chance to say two sentences, what will they be? ▪

It is important to go through the exercise described in checklist 57 in order to prepare what you want to say. But there is an important caveat. When you are interviewed you must not sound as though you have learned what you want to say parrot-fashion. You must retain a flexible mind and be thoroughly aware of all the background issues surrounding your key points. And you must have thought through how to link your key points naturally to any likely questions – hostile or otherwise – that may be asked. Above all, when faced with the task of doing a broadcast interview you must, no matter how short the proposed interview, prepare thoroughly what you want to say.

How to control your nerves before the interview starts
The success or failure of an interview is often determined before it starts. Partly, this is in the briefing and planning. Partly, it's in the care you take in presenting yourself. And, partly, it's in the mental attitude with which you approach the interview.

It is no use pretending you won't be nervous. Most people are nervous before an important event. Even skilled interviewees, who've been through the mill dozens of times, get nervous. And so, it must be said, do some of the interviewers!

Not all nervousness is bad. That tingle of anticipation which gets the adrenaline pumping in just the right quantities is likely to give you the edge to perform at your best. (In fact, if you weren't even a little bit nervous, that might be a cause for concern.) But over-whelming nervousness, complete with the three Ss – stammers, stutters and the shakes – is destructive. And you must do something to control it. The best place to start is by analysing the cause of the nervousness.

First, it is the worry of the unknown. But you will have overcome that by collecting all the information about the interview, the circumstances surrounding it and what is expected of you.

Second, it is the fear of failure. You will have tackled that worry by briefing yourself thoroughly on the subject of the interview. You will know the three points you want to get across. You will have chosen the outline form of words that will best get them across – complete with examples. You will be thoroughly briefed on the background facts. You will have considered the difficult questions that could be asked – and have your counters ready.

Third, it is the anticipation. It is the time spent sitting in the trenches that builds nervousness not going over the top. So before setting off for the studio, while travelling to it, and while waiting for the interview to start, you need things to keep you occupied. For example, you will want to look over your briefing materials so that they are completely fresh in your mind. Checklist 58 sets out some other things you can do to combat the physical symptoms of nervousness. Then, more positively, checklist 59 sets out some things you can do to prepare for an interview with confidence.

Checklist 58: six ways to combat nervousness before an interview

• Think positive. Don't get into a negative frame of mind. Your preparation should give you confidence.

- Breathe deeply. Your body needs oxygen to function at maximum efficiency. Steady breathing makes you feel better.
- Take a brisk walk. It burns up the adrenaline which is helping to make you feel nervous. And it tunes up your body.
- Loosen your face muscles. It is important that your face should be animated. So before the interview try "silent yawning" exercises. And loosen your neck and shoulder muscles with circular shoulder movements.
- Stop your hands shaking. Clench and unclench your fists to control your hand and wrist muscles.
- Note the position of the lavatory. If your nervousness makes you want to use it more than normal, knowing where it is removes some of the anxiety. ■

Checklist 59: 12 ways to prepare for a broadcast interview with confidence

- Consider your appearance. Television is largely about images. If you are only on screen for a minute or two, or possibly only a few seconds, most people may only remember the impression you left rather than your specific message. That impression is partly created by what you look like and partly by how you conducted yourself on screen. So does your appearance present you in the way you would like people to visualise you?
- Dress appropriately. Many of the old rules – suit and tie – have gone out of the window in the past few years. But it pays to give some thought to what to wear. Your clothes and accessories will make a statement about the kind of person you are. Whatever you decide, try to avoid patterns with

fine detail which tend to strobe on the screen. Bright white clothing doesn't always look good either. Women often score by wearing strong colours like red, blue or yellow.

- Get there in plenty of time. Allow time for finding a parking place, and for meeting your interviewer beforehand. You don't want to be hanging around for a long time before your interview – that builds unhelpful tension. But you don't want to rush in at the last moment out of breath and sweating.

- Meet the people involved in the interview. That is helpful in getting their measure before they start to interview. It can also be of value in helping them to rectify any errors or misconceptions they may have had about you before you go on air or on screen.

- Find out how you'll be introduced. In a panel discussion, studio interview or similar programme, find out the exact words the programme presenter will use to introduce you. Sometimes, they will volunteer this information. It is by no means unusual for errors to creep in, and it can be awkward if they're not sorted out before the interview starts.

- Probe the interviewer's line of questioning. Try to find out if the interviewer is going to adopt a particular slant. Sometimes that slant may be unhelpful and you may be able to persuade the interviewer to amend it. In any event, you will be forewarned.

- Ask the interviewer the exact words of the first question. He/she might not tell you. But if he/she does you will be able to fashion your first answer to fit the question. Often, the first question will be probing or even hostile. But don't plan to chase after all the negative nuances in it (although correct anything that is blatantly wrong). Instead, plan to put your own positive line.

- But keep your own counsel. Don't reveal what you intend to say before the interview starts. If you reveal your bull points to the interviewer, he/she may think of questions that undercut what you had planned to say.

- Accept make-up. It can make a significant difference to your on-screen image by removing the appearance of moist upper lips, jowly jaw-lines and shiny foreheads, etc.

- Don't bother about technicalities. It is not your job to worry about whether the interviewer's tape recorder is working properly or whether the lights are in the right place. Leave that to the experts and concentrate on your own performance.

- Consider illustrating to illuminate where appropriate. People may remember a telling example or brief story. In the case of a television interview about a simple product, consider showing it – holding it up in front of the camera might aid brand recognition. Avoid any prop that would distract from your main messages or is complex, organic, or alive, particularly if it might run off or bite!

- Beware of "hospitality" . At some studios you'll be offered drinks beforehand. Stick to one (small) one. Or better still none. You may think alcohol will give you Dutch courage. But the signs of drink show up very quickly on television – in your eyes. A drink of sweet tea will increase your blood sugar level and moisten a (possibly) dry mouth. ■

How to perform well in a broadcast interview

The key features of television news and – to a certain extent documentary programmes – are that they are fast-moving, concerned with visual images and controversial. (Controversy makes good television.) Because radio has only sound to convey its message, it is not concerned with visual images and there is normally more time to make points verbally. But background sound can also help to create either a positive or negative image. Like television, radio can be fast-moving and controversial.

You should pay special attention to the points in checklist 60 in order to improve your performance in broadcast interviews. (Not all the points apply to radio, but it is obvious which do.)

Checklist 60: 12 ways to perform well in a broadcast interview

- Get off to a good start. The first answer is crucially important, especially in a short interview. But in any interview it will set a standard by which your audience will judge you. That's why it is important to know what the first question will be, if at all possible, and to fashion your answer in advance.

- Be sincere and truthful. Television, with its probing eye, exposes insincerity mercilessly. You must believe in what you say. You must be truthful. If you can't do both those things, much better not to appear on television at all.

- Ignore distractions. In a studio there will be people all around you, doing their jobs, moving equipment, signalling to one another. Ignore them. Don't even try to catch what they're doing out of the corner of your eye. Focus your attention solely on your interviewer.

- Talk to the interviewer. He or she is asking you questions. Your answers should be addressed back to the interviewer. Or in a panel discussion to the chairperson. Don't talk to the camera. Or worse still, a vague spot somewhere in the studio. But, remember, as you talk to the interviewer, you are really talking through him or her to the audience beyond. And your answers should be fashioned with that in mind.

• Don't let the interviewer bully you. He or she may be asking you probing or even downright hostile questions. Don't be intimidated. Stand up for yourself. Put your point of view forcefully but fairly. Do not be goaded into losing your temper or cheap abuse. You gain points with the viewer or listener by keeping cool and collected under fire. On the other hand, don't adopt a matey tone with the interviewer or become obsequious so that you appear a crawler, bootlicker or toad. Keep your relationship formal and business-like.

• Be serious. In an interview about a serious subject, you should treat all questions seriously. Don't assume any questions have been flippant – even if they sound it. Answer questions with good humour but don't try to be funny in a forced way: that almost always back-fires.

• Don't make off-the-cuff comments. You should have prepared what you want to say beforehand. Stick to it. Don't introduce points you've just thought of. Avoid the temptation to make policy on your feet. Especially avoid making instantaneous analogies. They may contain shades of meaning you hadn't considered and give a wrong – perhaps seriously wrong – impression.

• Firmly correct any inaccuracies. Do not let any important factual inaccuracies from the interviewer or anyone else taking part in the programme go unchallenged. Otherwise the viewer will assume they are correct. Generally, make the correction in the first words you say as soon as it is your turn to speak. (It is only a good idea to interrupt in exceptional circumstances, but if the interviewer is saying something wrong you could indicate your disagreement by shaking your head. The viewer could see that, as well.)

- Look relaxed. Even if you aren't! Give yourself a quick visual check just before the interview starts to make sure hair is in place, tie straight, jacket buttoned, and so on. If doing the interview standing, don't fidget from one foot to another. Hold your arms in a relaxed fashion at your side. Make hand gestures naturally, where appropriate, but keep them under control. If sitting, sit up straight with legs together. Don't wriggle in your seat. In an interview close-up move your head a reasonable amount, but try to keep your body fairly still.

- Sound interested. If you don't sound as though you're interested in what you're saying, nobody else will be. That means keeping the voice bright and fresh. But avoid histrionics.

- Avoid distractions which might command the audience's attention. Don't play with your nose on camera, or sniff, rattle keys, or tap your pen on the table in front of a microphone. Doodling during a panel discussion can portray a lack of respect for others. Remember also that camera operators may be looking for "reaction shots" to edit in while others are speaking. If you chew gum, spit it out before the interview starts.

- Finish strongly. Know the length of the interview and judge when it is coming to a close. Get a strong bull point into your last answer – if necessary by repeating in new words something you have already said. ▪

In addition to the general points in the previous section, which apply to both television and radio, it is advisable to bear in mind the points in checklist 61 if you are involved in a television interview.

Checklist 61: eight special points to consider in a television interview

- Look at the interviewer. You are having a conversation with him or her. Don't glance about you. The movement of your eyes is especially noticeable on a television screen. If you keep looking around, you will either look stupid, uninterested or devious.

- Sit upright. Don't slump. But be comfortable. Let your hands rest in your lap.

- Project your personality. You don't want to go over the top. But if you are too "laid back" you'll just seem flat and the viewer will lose interest in what you're saying.

- Don't take notes. It's distracting. All the information you need should be in your head.

- Be alert at all times. The camera could switch to you at any moment.

- Control irritating mannerisms. If you wiggle your ears or have other annoying habits – don't. And try not to touch your face too much. It doesn't look good on screen.

- Be aware of time. You should know how long your interview is due to last. Be aware when it is ending so you can finish on a strong point.

- Listen carefully for question changes during "cutaways" . During recorded interviews the interviewer will re-record some of his/her questions after the interview is finished. That's because the camera has been on you during the interview. Listen carefully for any changes in the question on this re-filming. Sometimes reporters "harden" the question which can have an adverse effect on the answer you have just given.

Don't be afraid to protest loudly if this happens. ▪

You could be asked to do an interview from a remote studio. In this case, you will find yourself in a room with a camera pointing at you. You'll hear the interviewer's questions over a loudspeaker or through an earplug. In this case, talk to the camera. Treat it as a person. Make your face react to the question. (But don't pull faces!) The camera will often be on you while it is being asked. Speak in a normal conversational tone.

During a radio interview, bear in mind the additional points in checklist 62.

Checklist 62: six special points to consider in a radio interview

- Explain clearly what you mean. Remember that you can't use visual face signals to hint at your meaning, as with television, so make your voice convey your personality and mood.
- Keep your answers sharp and to the point. It's very easy to edit the tape of a radio interview. And this will happen if you ramble.
- Do your interview somewhere quiet. A lot of background noise can be distracting. Unless the noise is actually adding "location colour" to the piece.
- Don't make unnecessary noise. While being interviewed in a studio, don't rustle paper, bang on the table, knock the table leg or make other background noises. They are amplified on radio and sound awful.
- Call back if asked to do a telephone interview. It gives you time to gather your thoughts.
- If involved in a phone-in programme, listen carefully to

the questions through your headphones. Gently flatter the questioners, even when they're stupid. Give your answers in a conversational way. Never lose your temper.

The advice we've been discussing so far — both with print and broadcast journalists — is designed to carry you through most interviews. But there may be times when some of the normal rules go out of the window — when a genuine crisis occurs. And, then, you need to be prepared to deal with the worst.

Chapter 9

Communicating in a crisis

Why crisis communication is different

It can't happen to us. It can. That is why crisis communication skills are important to most organisations' spokespeople.

Of course, nobody wants a crisis. And most organisations plan to ensure they never get one. But at some stage in its life an organisation may face some sort of crisis. Of course, "crises" come in all shapes and sizes. The worst have tragic consequences when people die, as in a major transport accident. Others involve widespread problems with products, such as a product recall. Still others could involve an employee of an organisation being caught in questionable or even criminal conduct. And, then again, the organisation could be targeted by activists over some real or perceived grievance.

Some organisations are more vulnerable to crises than others. They include companies in the transport industry, companies handling or processing dangerous commodities such as chemicals or oil, companies with intrinsically dangerous manufacturing processes, or those providing mass consumer goods or food products where faulty merchandise could harm customers. Government departments and other public bodies, such as NHS trusts, are also prone to crises. Charities and not-for-profit bodies are not immune – especially those whose heroic staff work in dangerous parts of the world.

And even those not included on that list could face crises.

Their offices or factory could be burned down. They could be the victim of a major robbery or fraud. They could be on the receiving end of a hostile take-over bid. There could be law-suits or major computer failures to cope with. Unfortunately, a state of crisis has become a regular feature of modern life.

This chapter does not set out to show you how to draw up a complete crisis plan. That is a broader job that should involve a wide range of managers within the organisation, including those at the very top. Instead, this chapter concentrates on the communications aspects of the crisis plan and the spokesperson's role in it. So how is a crisis different from other kinds of corporate communication?

First, crisis news is bad news. It is about something that is likely to have an adverse effect on your organisation. Secondly, people may get hurt. The crisis is often about something that endangers or damages third parties – physically, emotionally or financially – not invariably, but in many cases. Sometimes, as we have noted, the crisis tragically involves injury or death to employees, customers or others.

Thirdly, you can't usually keep quiet about a crisis. No matter how much you might want to hush it up, it's going to be news. Other people know about it. Journalists will cover the story. And there's nothing you can do about that fact.

Fourthly, you can be on the wrong end of the law. Increasingly, your organisation or some of its managers could find themselves involved in civil or even criminal proceedings as a result of what has happened. Tougher legislation in many fields and a greater willingness by the courts to pin the blame of liability on organisations and the people who run them make this more likely.

As a result of all these factors, your organisation ought to have a crisis plan prepared – and part of that plan should be a crisis communication plan. The company spokesperson must be a member of the crisis planning team and have anticipated what may be required, from a communications perspective, in a given situation. Because you won't have time to prepare when trouble strikes, you must have done your preparation for general or generic crisis communication well in advance.

In fact, your preparation for crisis starts with the honest, open and ethical way you run your organisation. If your organisation has by its actions over the years developed a good reputation, it will be in a far stronger position to deal with a crisis when it comes. You will have already built up a bank of goodwill on which you can draw. A particular event could then be seen as an exception to the rule or bad luck for a well-managed organisation, rather than as evidence of general poor management or slack procedures.

In fact, a well thought-out and managed communication campaign over the years will also help to build the kind of image for your organisation that can take severe buffeting from the very occasional crisis event. Just as a court of law looks with greater favour on a transgressor of previous good character, so the public at large is prepared to make allowances for a company that has a favourable image.

How careful planning helps you deal with a crisis

Careful planning can't always avert a crisis, but it may contain it. It can help to avoid a "crisis within a crisis" – the panic that grips an organisation when it doesn't know what to do or when events develop their own self-propelled momentum and seem to spiral out of control. What planning can do is to anticipate and possibly channel the shock-waves of a crisis.

The starting point when you begin to plan is to identify the danger "hot spots" in your organisation. In management language, you need to conduct a risk assessment. It's time to think the unthinkable. What really could go wrong in your worst nightmares? Face up to it. What would you do if it happened? Checklist 63 lists questions that may help you to identify the "hot spots" in your own organisation.

Checklist 63: 15 questions to ask when identifying potential crisis hot spots

- What could happen?
- How could it happen?
- Where might it happen?
- When might it happen?
- Who would be directly affected?
- What about the indirect effects?
- Who else would be concerned?
- What criticism could we face?
- And from which quarters?
- Would laws be broken?
- What would we need to do to put it right?
- And who would need to be involved in doing so?
- And how much would it cost?
- Could we afford that kind of money?
- Frankly, could we cope?

By asking and answering the questions in checklist 63, you should have identified the issues that need to be resolved when you draw up a crisis plan. It is not, of course, the task of the organisation's spokesperson (or people) to take sole responsibility for drawing up a crisis plan. But the spokesperson should have considerable input on those elements of the plan that will involve dealing with the media.

And be in no doubt about how important that is in your crisis planning. To a large extent, when crisis strikes you will be judged not by how you deal with the crisis, but by how you are *seen* to be dealing with the crisis. In some instances, a badly handled response can trigger a more severe crisis than the initial catalyst. It is all too easy to get dragged into a situation where you have to devote great effort to "explaining away" unfortunate comments already made. Naturally, that is a distraction from getting to grips with the underlying problem.

So, remember, your response to a crisis – what you say and what you do – can be as newsworthy and as potentially damaging as the original crisis.

As a spokesperson, you will need to be certain that all the back-up you need will be in place should you be called on to perform during a crisis. Depending on the precise nature of the crisis you face, there are three areas that you should give particular attention to in your advance crisis planning.

1 *Agree on how the crisis will be managed.* Because every crisis is different, it is difficult to be prescriptive about how each should be managed beyond stating broad principles. It goes without saying that senior management – those responsible for running the organisation at the highest level – should be involved. How involved depends on the size of the organisation and the nature of the crisis. Perhaps they will be involved in a hands-on way, perhaps only in a policy-setting way. It is also necessary to decide where the crisis will be managed. Again, different crises demand different

responses. In some cases, where the crisis is a physical event, such as a major accident or a fire, there may be a case for managing the crisis close to the incident – bearing in mind that the immediate location, as in the case of an arson or terrorist attack, may be sealed off for forensic, safety or security reasons. On other occasions, where the crisis doesn't have such a specific location, it is probably more sensible to locate the crisis team in one of the organisation's offices, perhaps its main office. Whatever the arrangements, the crisis spokesperson needs to be part of them.

Many organisations conduct regular disaster planning, mapping out possible crisis scenarios and compiling contingency plans for dealing with them. It goes without saying that a contingency plan needs to be put in writing. In addition, every person responsible for an aspect of the plan needs to know clearly what their responsibilities will be in advance. The plan needs to be tested. As a crisis spokesperson, you need to be certain in advance that you will have a plan to mobilise the resources you need. Again, it is impossible to be definitive about resources but they may include:

- Extra staff support. To ensure that calls from journalists can be fielded, if necessary, around the clock. (Journalists don't keep office hours, and journalists from overseas – in different time zones – may also be calling you.)

- A call-out plan. To make sure you can get hold of all the people you need at any hour of the day or night, any day of the year.

- Procedures and processes that ensure necessary and relevant resources and information can be accessed and routed to you as and when needed.

- A "quiet room". Away from the bustle of the main activity, where you can draft statements and press releases and consider your next moves.

2 *Consider setting up a crisis press centre.* Whether you need or decide to set up a crisis press centre depends on the size of your organisation and the nature of the crisis. The guiding principle is how much media interest the crisis is likely to generate and what you regard as the best way of managing the response to that media interest. In a crisis, you may be deluged with requests for information from journalists. On the other hand, you may receive only a few desultory calls if the crisis turns out not to grab media attention. But, for the sake of this discussion, let's assume the crisis does grab the media. As a result, you may need to hold press conferences and you will need somewhere to hold them. You will also score brownie points with journalists if you make it easier for them to file stories by doing such things as providing telephones and computers with e-mail and internet access.

It is possible that your press centre will be at your head office. But it may be nearer the site of the crisis incident (if there was a single site). If you foresee that a particular site – perhaps a plant or depot – could possibly be the site of a crisis, you may want to make contingency arrangements with a near-by hotel, hall or branch office to provide accommodation at short notice for a press centre in the event of the worst happening.

In general, you should try to avoid setting up the crisis press centre actually at the site of the incident. That can be too close for comfort. Even half a mile away can provide the distance that somehow enables both company spokespeople and journalists to develop a sense of proportion about what has happened. Checklist 64 provides an *aide memoire* for the sort of facilities you could need in the crisis press centre.

Checklist 64: 14 facilities needed in a crisis press centre

- Telephones (and extra lines, if necessary)
- Telephone recording equipment (to tape key phone calls)
- Computers with internet and e-mail access
- Fax machine
- Television(s)
- Video recorder/DVD (to record coverage of incident)
- Radio(s)
- Tape recorders (to tape radio coverage)
- Audio visual aids (to explain background to incident)
- Desks, tables, chairs and other relevant furniture
- Corporate set (background for press conferences. Not essential but increasingly used by many organisations.)
- Stationery
- Tea, coffee and soft drinks
- Quiet room (for broadcast interviews) ▩

You should remember that you may need to transport much of the equipment to site. So it needs to be readily accessible. And transport must be instantly available.

3 *Draft a briefing kit to use in the event of a crisis.* You won't have time to draft all the background documentation you will need if a crisis strikes, so you should prepare in advance general background on your organisation and its key players that may be useful in a crisis. The media may be hungry for information about your organisation and what it does – including products or services affected by the incident – its managers and any installations or other of the organisation's activities that are directly involved. Having this background information readily to hand will make

your life a lot easier should your organisation hit trouble.

Normally, it might seem hard work trying to get journalists interested in your organisation and what you do. But when a crisis strikes, it can seem as though every media newshound in the country and beyond is after the information. So you need to be in a position to start providing information about your organisation within minutes of a crisis occurring.

Checklist 65: five kinds of information to include in a crisis briefing kit

- Details of the incident in bald, factual terms as far as is definitely known, together with what action the organisation has already taken.
- Background to the organisation.
- Background to the installation involved in the crisis (if there is a specific installation), what it does and the benefits it provides to the local community and more broadly.
- Background to product(s) involved in the incident (if relevant), who uses them and the benefits they provide
- Details of senior people involved in managing the organisation and the crisis incident.

Apart from the information mentioned in checklist 65, you should also identify those media or special interest groups that are likely to display concern if a given crisis occurs. It is important to know who and how many journalists are likely to want information about the incident. And it is also important to know how to contact people such as political and community leaders, public officials and others who may want up-to-date information about the crisis.

How to get fair-minded people on your side in a crisis

It is when a crisis strikes that your organisation is most likely to provoke critics – and when it most needs friends. It would be naive to imagine that you can disarm all your critics in a crisis. People with an axe to grind will always find reason to carp. And a crisis tends to make your organisation a target for the release of pent up feelings. But if you do the right things, you should win a hearing from fair-minded people. A crucial test of your success in crisis communications is whether you are winning or losing the support of those fair-minded and unbiased people of goodwill.

Many of the points mentioned earlier in this book apply as much in crisis communications as in other kinds of communications. But there are special features of crisis communications that you need to be aware of. So when a crisis strikes you need to be:

1 *First with the news.* It's your crisis – and don't let anyone take it away from you! You must demonstrate that you are aware of what is happening. And if, in the early hours of the crisis, you are short of hard news, you should seek to fill the gap with relevant background material. By giving the press some facts, you may reduce their temptation to speculate unhelpfully.

2 *The authoritative source of information.* You need to be the source from which the media gets the facts first. To do that, you need to demonstrate openness. You need to be truthful and accurate. And you have to be prepared to release information as and when it becomes available. To do otherwise risks encouraging the media to seek other sources of information – sources that may be hostile to you. At the same time, while being helpful with information, you should rigorously avoid speculation about what might be happening. "It's too early to say…" might be the true response and could be seen as reasonable and responsible.

3 *Proactive in your response to the crisis.* That means, not only being open and timely in releasing information about an incident. It means providing information as soon as possible about what you are going to do to rectify the situation. But don't hand hostages to fortune. Stick to the facts and what is actually about to be "delivered". In order to be first with the news, the authoritative source of information and pro-active in its provision, you may need to hold regular press conferences. But, depending on the circumstances, it may be sufficient to brief journalists in informal groups or individually. It helps to demonstrate you are willing to communicate. And it takes pressure off your spokespeople by staunching the flow of calls to the press centre from journalists. For every press conference prepare thoroughly using the guidelines in checklists 28 and 41. Set a reasonable time limit. Close the conference decisively when journalists have had a fair opportunity to ask their questions. Try to arrange for your spokespeople to leave by a separate exit from the journalists to avoid them being pursued by reporters, camera crews and photographers. But don't give the impression that they're slinking away.

At press conferences, and in other meetings both with the media and others involved in the crisis, you should be concerned and compassionate. You must demonstrate that you sympathise with people who have suffered as a result of the incident. Say so in any statement you make. Show real human warmth and understanding for their travail. Don't appear cold and calculating. If you try "smart" explanations in an attempt to shift the blame, you could alienate many people who recognise that accepting responsibility and showing sympathy is a more courageous and human response.

But, at the same time, you should be able to refute false

accusations about your organisation or the incident. In a crisis, accusations can start to fly. They need to be put down as firmly as you know how (but whenever possible without rancour), and as swiftly as possible. To leave accusations unanswered, allows them to fester and become part of the mythology of an incident. The best way to put down accusations is with irrefutable facts. You need to make sure that any facts you need are going to be readily available.

4 *Keep everyone affected by the crisis informed.* That may mean keeping in direct contact with employees and families of employees or with customers. It also may mean keeping in direct contact with local councils, MPs and local communities. You will be building goodwill after an incident by showing you are helpful and accessible to people who may have an interest or may take a view of the situation.

5 *Match your emotions and message with the mood of the moment.* You need to demonstrate that you are aware of the feelings of people involved in the incident. You need to be more than a reciter of facts and figures about your company and the incident. You must demonstrate an appropriate emotional response in what you do and say.(But that doesn't mean you should indulge yourself with insincere hand-wringing.) You need to be totally sincere and honest about your emotional response in order that what you say rings true.

To coin a rather time-worn advertising slogan, there is no need to make a drama out of a crisis.

Chapter 10

How to do even better next time

Evaluating the results of your efforts

If you are to be effective as a spokesperson, you will need to evaluate the impact of what you are doing in order to assess its value, identify any matters that may need to be corrected or otherwise put right, and find ways of improving your performance. In performing this task you need to look at two issues:

1 *Your personal performance as a spokesperson.* You should be as objective as possible about your own performance as a spokesperson. And, where possible, you should invite the constructive comments of helpful and trusted colleagues on your performance.

After every interview try to answer the questions in checklist 66 as honestly as possible. (You might ask your trusted colleagues the same questions.)

Checklist 66: 10 questions to ask after an interview

- Did I manage to get across my main message during the interview?
- If not, had I thought through the main message clearly enough?
- Did I explain my points in simple and straightforward language?
- Did I pitch my comments at the right level for the audience I was trying to reach?

- Was my message backed with convincing facts?
- Did I use enough illuminating examples?
- Did the interview serve either a specific objective or the broader aims of the organisation?
- Did my appearance and manner present an appropriate image for our organisation?
- What, if anything, should I do differently next time?
- What else do I need to do to improve my performance as a spokesperson? ▪

If you answer "no" to any of the first eight questions in checklist 66, you need to consider what you can do next time to improve that aspect of your performance – and you should also have material to help you answer the last two questions.

2 *The impact of your efforts as a spokesperson upon your organisation's objectives.* In assessing this you need to be both objective and realistic. First, you need to appreciate that the media's primary purpose is not to help you achieve your organisation's objectives. If necessary, refer back to chapter three about what the media want in order to remind yourself about how they approach interviews and what drives journalists.

Secondly, most people do not read every article in every newspaper and magazine to which they subscribe with obsessive attention to detail. Nor do they necessarily pay rapt attention to every word you utter on television or radio. In general, they tend to gain a "general impression". (If you asked someone to name three specific stories from yesterday's newspaper, they would probably be hard put to do it.) Today's newspaper is tomorrow's fish and chip wrapping. So, in general, it is advisable to look at what has been written from the point of view of a mildly interested outsider.

Would that outsider grasp the main thrust of your message? Would he or she generally think better of your organisation as a result of reading the article?

Don't be obsessed with minor errors of fact or subtle nuances of meaning which you think the writer has missed. The mildly interested reader is not going to be obsessed by them. Of one thing you can be certain: minor errors will occur frequently. In many cases, although regrettable, they don't make much difference to the overall main thrust of your message. So keep a sense of proportion about them.

Similarly, the interviewer may present your views in a slightly different way to that which you had hoped. Again, keep your feet on the ground. Be objective. Has the main point of your message really been missed? If not, you have probably achieved your main objective.

However, if an error does make a material difference to the way your organisation is presented or how people, including those with specialised knowledge, might perceive it, that is a different matter and you should seek to correct it. In these cases, the detail of the presentation and the editorial line the publication or programme has taken can be more important. But remember that if you become too obsessive about what is written about your organisation, you will fail to see the broader issues involved, you will rapidly become discouraged with your media communications, and you will fail to achieve the many positive benefits that can flow from a constructive dialogue with the media.

In relating the results of media communications activity to business objectives, you need to develop relevant measures of success and machinery for monitoring those measures. So before we come on to consider what you should do if you have to correct an error, let's look at the important matter of how to evaluate the overall impact of your media communications.

How to measure the impact you make

In measuring the results of your activities as a spokesperson, there are two main issues you need to address. First, how much media coverage you achieved – and whether it was helpful. Second, whether that coverage moved your organisation closer to achieving any of its objectives. The first is easier to measure than the second – but, with a certain amount of thought and ingenuity the second can also usefully be monitored.

First, how much coverage have your activities generated?

There are three main approaches that you can adopt. They contain varying degrees of sophistication and may or may not be relevant depending on the precise circumstances of your campaign. They are:

1 *Column centimetres.* A crude measure, but one that can give you a warm feeling if there are plenty of cuttings. (For broadcast coverage, substitute minutes for centimetres.) The trouble is, not all coverage carries the same weight or is of equal value. And some of the coverage may not be positive. Some of it may not even be as a result of your activities. But don't write off column centimetres completely. They are proof that you have been doing something – and that it has had a result.

2 *Audience-related coverage.* You measure the coverage you get against the likely proportion of your target audience reached by the media carrying the coverage. There is no precisely scientific way of doing this. But by collating details of the circulation profiles of publications in which material about your organisation appears, and matching them against the total size of your audience, you can

get a fair measure of whether you are hitting the right media.

3 *Advertising equivalent value.* This is not so much a way of measuring the quantity of coverage as its perceived value.

It is possible to calculate the advertising value equivalent of the press coverage received using the rate cards of the relevant publications or the industry reference guide, BRAD. The benefit of this approach is that it puts a cash value on the results of your media campaign. This approach does have the merit of attaching different weights to different publications – through the variation in their advertising rates. But it suffers from some of the same faults as measuring column centimetres. Your organisation may have a small mention in a larger piece and it takes no account of positive or negative coverage. Moreover, most publications discount their advertising rate cards, sometimes heavily, so that calculations using the rate cards give an unrealistically high value to the coverage you've received.

Secondly, has the coverage helped to achieve your objectives.

This is a much tougher question to answer because it involves going beyond how much coverage you and your organisation have received to what impact it has had on the people you were trying to reach. There is no one approach to doing this and it may be that a combination of approaches work best. A starting point could be trying to evaluate the value of the coverage in a way that determines whether it was helpful or unhelpful. In doing this, there are two techniques which you may want to consider – weighted evaluation of your media coverage and market research.

1 *Media evaluation.* In the last few years, there has been a considerable growth in the number of specialist companies which offer more sophisticated ways of measuring the value of media coverage. The companies have formed their own industry

association, the Association of Media Evaluation Companies (www.amec.org.uk).

This growth has taken place largely because the more sophisticated users of media relations realised that they needed to discover just how far their media coverage was supporting their organisation's objectives or the objectives of specific media campaigns. These specialists have developed sophisticated methodologies designed to evaluate the value of media coverage. The methodology each company uses is unique but it is likely to take account of issues such as the publication in which the coverage appears, the size of the coverage, its position in the publication, whether the organisation's name is mentioned in a headline or standfirst (the copy, usually set in larger type, that introduces an article), whether there are pictures, whether the coverage is favourable or unfavourable to the organisation's or campaign's objectives, whether rival organisations are mentioned alongside it and so on. By giving weights to all of these factors and using an algorithm to calculate them, it's possible to produce a measure which, in theory at least, defines how closely your organisation is getting to achieving its objectives through media coverage.

This approach is certainly much more sophisticated than merely measuring column inches or calculating advertising equivalent values. Yet the measures the evaluation company calculate depend on the methodology and algorithm it uses. Whether that provides a true indication of the value your organisation receives from the coverage is open to debate. Perhaps a different methodology would produce a different measure. In short, the value of this approach depends on agreeing at the outset what the methodology should be and that it will provide a reliable indicator of the value of media coverage.

And, at the end of the day, while the measurement you get may tell you what the media think about your organisation and its activities, it doesn't tell you how far that coverage has shaped public perceptions about what your organisation does.

2 *Market research.* To find out what people think, you may want to consider doing some market research. The Market Research Society (www.mrs.org.uk), can provide lists of market research firms that perform attitude surveys. The specialists can help you design a survey which should provide you with information about the positive and negative perceptions people have of your organisation. But, of course, regular market research is not an inexpensive option. And each survey is only a snapshot in time of public attitudes towards your organisation. To know whether those perceptions are improving or declining, you need to repeat the research at regular intervals.

Another problem is to know just how far public perceptions about your organisation are shaped by what people read in the media and how much by other factors – such as their personal experience of using your products or services or dealing with your staff. To some extent, a skilled market research firm can design a piece of research to filter out these other factors, but this is not a precise science.

As you can see, it is not easy to find a precisely scientific way of measuring the contribution of a media communications campaign to specific objectives. Clearly, the inter-play of different forces affecting the achievement of any given objective can be so complex that it is often impossible to separate out precisely the influence of one from another.

But you can often find some measure of success. The starting point is to apply a simplified version of a methodology that has been widely used by some companies to measure their total business success – the use of "critical success factors" and "key performance indicators". The key to using this methodology successfully in measuring the impact of media communications is to choose relevant critical success factors for each objective. Then you have to find a realistic key performance indicator or indicators for each critical success factor. That can best be explained by giving two examples:

New product launch: If you launch a new product, a critical success factor might be how many you will sell in year one. A key performance indicator of whether you are likely to achieve that is how many enquiries you receive about it from qualified prospective purchasers each sales quarter.

Membership recruitment: If your critical success factor is to increase the number of members in your organisation, a key performance indicator could be how many enquiries you receive about membership each month.

As you can see, each objective should have its own critical success factor(s) which, in turn, require relevant key performance indicator(s). When you have decided which key performance indicators you are going to measure, you will need to put in place a measurement process to collect the information. Checklist 67 sets out some of the ways in which you can collect the data on your key performance indicators.

Checklist 67: 10 ways to collect data about campaign performance

- Market research questionnaire
- Personal experience

- Telephone surveys
- Postal surveys
- E-mail surveys
- Website questionnaires/polls
- Contact centre or sales-force questions
- Question on application and other forms
- Desk research of existing performance data
- Focus (discussion) groups

In measuring the impact of media communications, no method is perfect. It is also important not to become paralysed by measurement or to devote disproportionate resources to it. But using reasonable measurement techniques concentrates the mind wonderfully on making sure that activity serves defined objectives. But the true effectiveness of any media communications can only be judged by assessing its impact on those factors that determine whether or not you achieve your organisation's objectives.

What to do when it all goes wrong

One thing you can be sure of: mistakes will happen. What you need to do is to keep a sense of proportion about these mistakes. There are various courses of action open to you for correcting mistakes, but before you embark on any of them you should ask yourself whether any real harm has been done.

You may well find yourself dealing with journalists from certain publications or radio and television stations that regularly cover your area. It doesn't help long-term relations to be carping continually about minor errors. Indeed, when something does go wrong, you should always start by asking whether it was possibly your fault. Did you explain it clearly enough? Did you provide the right information? A surprising number of "mistakes" in newspapers and magazines occur because journalists were given the "wrong" information.

If something has gone wrong, there are a number of possible ways to put it right. These are:

A "quiet word". Start by approaching the journalist who has made the mistake. The mistake may – often will – be completely innocent and he or she will be anxious to put it right. Your approach should be friendly rather than censorious. In some cases, you will find the journalist is pleased that you have approached him or her first rather than going direct to the editor. You may find the journalist willing to write a "follow-on" story in which the original error can be corrected as well as new information given. Clearly, if the journalist is unhelpful, and you feel the matter is sufficiently important, you must approach the editor for a correction.

A correction. You should ask for a correction where there has been a significant error of fact. When doing so, ask for the correction as soon as possible. Give the editor as much time as possible to get it into the next issue of the publication. And make sure your facts are absolutely correct when asking for the correction. But be certain the correction will not do more harm than good.

The editor may publish the correction in one of two ways. The first is as a formal correction, normally an item on the same or a near page to where the original article appeared. And the correction may or may not offer an apology according to whether or not any serious inconvenience or hurt was caused. The second way is as a follow-on story, what journalists call correcting the error "in passing". The journalist will mention the error in his new story and give the true facts. It will generally be done in a down-beat way.

Letter to the editor. You should use the letter to the editor where you feel that the publication has seriously misrepresented your point of view. (The letter to the editor can be used for serious errors of fact, but these are best dealt with by the method above.) When correcting what the writer has originally written, do so in a constructive way. And try to write without rancour or name-calling which does not normally enhance your case. Stick to the central issues where you feel misrepresented, and make sure your letter is crystal clear. Don't make it sound like a letter from a solicitor. Keep the tone polite and business-like.

Complaint to Press Complaints Commission. You can complain to the Press Complaints Commission (www.pcc.org.uk) when you feel a newspaper or magazine has not dealt with your complaint fairly or reasonably. The PCC's website contains a detailed Code of Conduct which sets out grounds for complaint. If you are planning to complain about an article, you should write to the PCC setting out the grounds of your complaint, enclosing a copy of the article and explaining what the newspaper or magazine has done (or not done) to meet your concerns. You need to make your representations to the PCC within two months of publication, unless the article remains on its website or unless there has been protracted correspondence with the publication's editor. In that event, you can take your case to the PCC two months after the end of the correspondence. The PCC's website sets out in detail how it handles complaints and what you would be expected to do at each stage of the process.

Complaints about a television or radio programme. If you want to complain about a television or radio programme, you should first send your complaint to the person responsible for the programme concerned. In the case of news broadcasts, this will be the editor. In the case of documentaries or other factual programming, it will be the producer. If your complaint concerns a BBC television or radio programme, the BBC has a website (www.bbc.co.uk/complaints/) which guides potential complainants through its complaints procedure. As a first port of call, ITV provides a feedback service (www.itv.com/page.asp?partid=1215) which can be the starting point for making a complaint. In cases of clear, demonstrable and major error, the broadcasting companies are normally prepared to broadcast a correction. But they are frequently unwilling to broadcast corrections for small but possibly significant errors.

Complaint to Ofcom. If you are not happy with the way your complaint has been handled by any UK broadcasting company, you can take your complaint to Ofcom. In 2005, Ofcom adopted a Broadcasting Code which sets out standards UK broadcasters have to follow and grounds for complaint. The code is to be found on Ofcom's website at www.ofcom.org.uk. The code is a detailed document but the sections which may be of most concern to organisations seeking to present their case in the broadcast media are section five, which deals with due impartiality, due accuracy and undue prominence of views, and section seven, which deals with fairness.

Issue a writ for libel. This is definitely a last resort. And you should not take action unless you consult a lawyer. Incidentally, when it comes to libel, it does no harm to consult one of the firms of specialist libel lawyers who still cluster around Fleet Street and the Royal Courts of Justice in The Strand even though the newspapers have left – the publication or broadcasters you are suing will probably be doing the same. You don't want to be out-gunned on the legal front. In order to prove libel, you have to establish that:

- What you're complaining about was actually published. In this context, published means also broadcast on radio, television, teletext or the internet.
- That it refers to you or your organisation. It doesn't necessarily have to refer to you by name, but you or your organisation must be recognisable from what is written.
- That what is written about you or your organisation is defamatory. Broadly, there are three tests as to whether something might be defamatory. They are whether what you complain of tends to lower you in the estimation of right-thinking members of society; whether it tends to bring you into hatred, ridicule, contempt, dislike or disesteem with those right-thinkers; whether it tends to make you shunned or avoided or cut off from the said right-thinkers.

You could find that the people you are suing for libel will try one of five defences:

- Justification: If what was written was true they have a complete answer to your charge of defamation.
- Fair comment: If the writer of the offending article can show that what was said was his or her honest opinion, made without malice, then you may lose your case.
- Privilege: Some things can be published and receive complete protection from suits for libel. They include reports of judicial proceedings and Parliamentary papers. Fair and accurate reports of them in publications also attract privilege. So, in some cases, do fair and accurate reports of public meetings.
- Section 4 of the Defamation Act. 1952. The publisher of the libel can claim that it was "innocent" – the publisher did not mean to publish the libel about you and did not know of the circumstances in which what was written referred to you. But

the publisher must have taken "reasonable care" and he must make a prompt offer of "amends" after his unwitting libel.

• Apology under Libel Acts, 1843 and 1845. Very rare. Only applies to newspapers and periodicals. The publisher must show that the libel got into the paper without malice or negligence and that he or she apologised or offered to apologise as soon as the mistake was realised.

But libel is certainly not something to embark upon lightly. A case can last for days, if not weeks, with vast costs. And even if you win, you may only score a Pyrrhic victory.

Now it's up to you

Well, that's it. You have finally come to the end of *How to Make Your Case in the Media*. If you have been through every page, you must be congratulated for your thoroughness. But where do you go from here?

First, you cannot expect to absorb every fact and piece of advice at once. From time to time, return to those chapters of the book that you feel are relevant to whatever work you have in hand.

Second, don't just put your copy of this book aside on a shelf to gather dust. It is intended as more than a once-only source of instruction. It should be a useful source of reference. You can use the checklists as ideal quick reminders before undertaking a particular media assignment.

Third, put the lessons you have learned into effect. It is not a detailed knowledge of theory, but practical experience that is going to make you a valuable spokesperson for your organisation.

Fourth, don't expect to achieve miracles overnight. Building a helpful image for your organisation and getting across its key messages takes time. And it requires persistence. So does building useful and productive media contacts. Don't be put off by the occasional rebuff.

Fifth, whatever your specialist activity – and it might, of course, be communications or public relations – you could find that the ability to communicate well-conceived and expressed messages will give a valuable boost to your career prospects.

Remember, we now live in the Age of the Communicator. Good luck.

Index